Until I Come

By Jim Hockaday

Until I Come

SCRIPTURE VERSION NOTATIONS

Unless otherwise indicated, all Scripture quotations are taken from the *King James Version* of the Bible.

Scripture quotations marked AMP are taken from *The Amplified Bible* (AMP). *The Amplified Bible, Old Testament*, Copyright © 1965, 1987 by The Zondervan Corporation. *The Amplified New Testament*, Copyright © 1958, 1987 by The Lockman Foundation. Used by permission.

Scripture quotations marked NIV are taken from *The Holy Bible, New International Version..* Copyright © 1973, 1978, 1984 by The International Bible Society. Used by permission of Zondervan bible Publishers. All rights reserved.

DEDICATION

With gratefulness to the Lord Jesus Christ and the assistance of the Holy Ghost, I dedicate this book to my beautiful wife, Erin, and my three daughters Alli, Drew, and Chloe. Thank you for constantly surrounding me with loving support and appreciation for my role as husband and father. You are a tremendous encouragement to me to obey the call of God for our lives. I love you forever and will always honor each of you.

I also thank God for loving and godly parents who faithfully commit their time to our family and ministry. Mom and Dad, I love you very much.

CONTENTS

Preface

One morning while I was praying with a small group of people, I had a very interesting experience. Prayer was going well; however, it lacked something. We joined hands and continued to pray. As we did, immediately I was in the Spirit.

The apostle John wrote about such an experience in Revelation 1:10: **I was in the Spirit on the Lord's day, and heard behind me a great voice, as of a trumpet.** The phrase "I was in the Spirit" is the same as saying "the Spirit overpowered me." This simply means that the spirit realm was very real to me at that moment—more so, in fact, than the natural or physical realm.

In this vision, I found myself standing before what appeared to be a very large bookshelf. It seemed as though this bookshelf was suspended in the middle of nothing, yet my surroundings seemed very celestial or heavenly. As I looked more intently, I noticed that there were many scrolls on the shelves. Each scroll was about twelve inches long and neatly placed on the shelves.

As I gazed at this enormous bookshelf, I had an inner knowing that I was to unroll as many scrolls as I could. So one after the other, I began to take the scrolls off the shelves, opening each one to read its contents. But each time before I could read any of the writings, the contents of the scroll were instantly imparted to my belly or spirit. As Proverbs 20:27 says, **The spirit of man is the candle of the LORD, searching all the inward parts of the belly.**

It seemed apparent to me in this vision that I would not be able to open all the scrolls, but still I continued. Meanwhile, I became aware of a figure approaching from my left. When I turned to look, I saw it was a horse with a rider. I continued to open as many scrolls as I could until the visitor had drawn near to me.

As I looked at the rider on the horse, I noted that he was not Jesus. His appearance seemed angelic. He was a messenger sent to give me a key and to provide information. (Angelic appearances occurred often in the beginning of the church age, and they will increase as we approach the end of the age.)

This angelic being placed his left hand inside his garment and pulled out what resembled a very small scroll. Then for the first time, he spoke to me, saying, "I have come to give the key that will unlock the mysteries you have partaken of. Take this and eat it."

The messenger then handed me the scroll. I took it out of his hand and put it in my mouth. I don't recall any particular taste to the scroll, yet I was very aware that it dissolved quickly and that I was able to swallow it.

Next, the messenger reached out with his left hand for my left arm. I could tell he was about to lift me onto the horse, and I allowed him to do so. The next thing I knew, we were riding away from the bookshelf. The environment that seemed so tranquil had suddenly changed into nighttime. We were now in the heavenlies.

As we rode, we ascended up a mountain. It was dark all around us. I could see stars as though I were out in the wilderness on a dark, clear night. When we reached the top of the mountain, the angel let me down and said, "What you have received, now declare."

Through this experience I was aware of standing alone, and I recognized that what I was commissioned to declare might be different from anything I had ever imagined. Yet I was also aware that the Lord would be with me, confirming His Word with signs following (Mark 16:20).

My purpose in sharing this account is not to influence your thinking as a result of my experience. Rather, my hope is that this vision—as with any spiritual experience—will be subject to and discerned by the counsel of God's Word so it can bring blessing to those who receive it.

I encourage you to open your heart as you examine closely the truth presented in this book and judge it according to the Word of God. I strongly believe that the message contained in the following pages provides some keys that will grant access into places and rooms in the realm of the Spirit where the body of Christ must operate if believers are to effectively do the works of Christ in the final hours before He comes.

INTRODUCTION

Time as we know it seems to be drawing to a close. Signs of the soon return of our Lord Jesus Christ are as broadly displayed as billboards with messages that are crystal clear. Never has a generation seen so much prophecy fulfilled. Yet our generation is poised at the brink of what is only the beginning of sorrows.

The title of this book, *Until I Come*, is drawn from the parable Jesus told in Luke 19:11-28. This parable refers to the diligence required of those disciples who actively await the return of the Lord. Verse 13 states, **And he called his ten servants, and delivered them ten pounds, and said unto them, Occupy till I come.** Simply put, Jesus said, "Busy yourselves in the work you have been commissioned to do."

Hebrews 11:6 NKJV tells us, **But without faith it is impossible to please Him, for he who comes to God**

must believe that He is, and that He is a rewarder of those who diligently seek Him. Luke writes that Jesus asked His disciples if anyone would be exercising their faith when He returned (See Luke 18:8).

Years ago while I was working for a management firm that provided services for health-care facilities, I learned an important lesson that applies here. On a certain occasion, I instructed a worker to sanitize a particular wing of a hospital. My instructions were very simple, requiring no further information—or so I thought.

When I returned to check on the job, I was shocked to discover that the individual who had been assigned this simple task was actually mopping the floor without using any water or disinfectant! When I inquired about the method he was using to "clean and sanitize" the hall, he replied, "You didn't tell me that I had to use any water or disinfectant."

At that moment, I learned a valuable truth: unless I described specifically and in detail what a particular job required, I could not expect the outcome to match my initial intent.

If the person doing the cleaning had continued to perform the job *his* way, the floor would have remained dirty and unsanitary. Not only that, but people would have wondered whether or not our company could actually handle the job entrusted to us. But if my instructions had been carefully given and followed, the job would have been carried out to completion. The quality of the job performed would have proven that my instructions had been followed and my purpose for that task had been effectively fulfilled.

Similarly, God the Father has a very specific and detailed plan for mankind. Jesus came to earth for the precise purpose of fulfilling this assignment. He succeeded thoroughly in this purpose, establishing all aspects of His victory by crossing every "t" and dotting every "i." Following His great triumph, Jesus delegated His authority to the church so His will could continue to be enforced on the earth.

In Romans 8:19 and 22, the apostle Paul says that all creation groans, waiting for the manifestation of the sons of God. *J. B. Phillip's* translation of verse 19 says, **The whole creation is on tiptoe to see the wonderful sight of the sons of God coming into their own.** In Clarence Jordan's words: **In fact, the fondest dream of the universe is to catch a glimpse of real live sons of God.**[1]

The world will not recognize the manifestation of the sons of God until we walk in and express the divine will of God openly. Jesus was a pure and identical expression of His Father; we are to be the expression of Christ. The world will believe and receive our presentation of the gospel message when we manifest the glory of God in a way they can see and experience.

It is my earnest prayer that the message of *Until I Come* will challenge you to obey Jesus's admonition in

Colossians 3:2 (MESSAGE): **Look up, and be alert to what is going on around Christ—that's where the action is. See things from his perspective.**

You see, unless you gain understanding of the earthly ministry of Jesus and of your ability and responsibility to duplicate His results, your aim will reach far below His high expectation for your life. Therefore, as you read this book, consider this: is what you believe producing results in your life and in the lives of others? If so, you will be inspired to step out beyond your self-imposed limits and do more.

But if you're not experiencing the power of God moving in and through your life, I encourage you to let go of your preconceived ideas and get ready for a ride to the other side. By the end of this book, I believe your heightened expectancy alone will produce God-desired results both for yourself and for others. Then as this age draws to a close, you will confidently await the Master's return, knowing that you have understood and effectively followed His command: *until I come,* the works that I do, you shall do also. (See John 14:12.)

Chapter 1

THE WORKS OF JESUS

During Jesus's earthly ministry, He performed many miraculous acts with great confidence and total authority. He challenged devils and religious leaders alike with the same unflinching boldness. But of all the assertions Jesus made in reference to His own ministry, none seem more outrageous than when He said, **Verily, verily, I say unto you, He that believeth on me, the works that I do shall he do also; and greater works than these shall he do: because I go unto my Father** (John 14:12).

Now, obviously the work of redemption was a work that Jesus alone could do. He alone as Divinity could pay the price of sin and purchase our salvation with His own sinless blood. But in His earthly ministry as a man anointed by the Holy Spirit, Jesus performed miracles and works of power so we could do the same.

The apostle John said that if every miracle Jesus ever

performed in His earthly ministry could be recorded, all the books of the world could not contain the information. (John 21:25.) So I ask you: If you really believed you could do the same works—and even greater works—than Jesus did, what would you do? How would you act? How would you conduct your daily life?

The Word: Key to God's Power

As the Scriptures state, the primary works Jesus performed on a regular basis were teaching, preaching, and healing. The church has spent most of its time emphasizing the first two elements of Jesus's ministry, giving little attention to His healing works. However, it is true that ministering the Word of God through teaching and preaching is the single most important thing believers must accept as their responsibility in order to carry out the works of Jesus on the earth.

We are all expected to share the good news of the gospel because **faith cometh by hearing, and hearing by the word of God** (Romans 10:17). The Word serves both as our instruction manual and our inspiration in the Christian lifestyle. Therefore, preaching the Word is the number one way to inspire faith, not only for salvation but also for experiencing the benefits of salvation.

In the gospel of John, we see that Jesus Himself is the Word of God:

> **In the beginning was the Word, and the Word was with God, and the Word was God.**
>
> **The same was in the beginning with God.**
>
> **All things were made by him; and without him was not any thing made that was made.**
>
>

John 1:1-3

This passage shows us the significance and the power of God's Word. In verse 14, John goes on to say:

> **And the Word was made flesh, and dwelt among us, (and we beheld his glory, the glory as of the only begotten of the Father,) full of grace and truth.**

In the same way, the Word of God will manifest the glory of God today when it is both proclaimed and received.

The Word of God is the number one prerequisite for experiencing a consistent demonstration of the power of God. This is the reason Jesus completely submitted to the words of His Father, as we see in John 12:49-50 NKJV:

> **"For I have not spoken on My own authority; but the Father who sent Me gave Me a command, what I should say and what I should speak.**
>
> **"And I know that His command is everlasting**

life. Therefore, whatever I speak, just as the Father has told Me, so I speak.”

Jesus recognized that the words of His Father not only had authority, but the power to back them up—divine power to impart everlasting life to all those who heard and received the truth. That's why Jesus was earlier quoted as saying, “The words that I speak are spirit, and they are life” (John 6:63).

You see, when Jesus walked on this earth, He did so as a man. He emptied Himself of any unique advantage to operate in this world so He could fully identify with man and become man's faithful high priest (Hebrews 2:17). Jesus lived on earth as a man filled with divine life, yet at the same time He was God's Son. The beauty of redemption is that as believers, we too, are filled with divine life and are called sons of God (1 John 3:1).

Jesus was extremely disciplined and submitted to the words of His Father, whether the spoken or the written Word of God. Thus, Jesus was successful in bringing the Word to light.

I love to read Matthew 8:16-17 in which Jesus **cast out the spirits with his word, and healed all that were sick: that it might be fulfilled which was spoken by Esaias the prophet, saying, Himself took our infirmities, and bare our sicknesses.** Notice how Jesus manifested the power of the Holy Spirit: He did so *according to what was already written.*

Second Timothy 3:16 says, **All scripture is given by inspiration of God, and is profitable for doctrine, for reproof, for correction, for instruction in righteousness.** Then in Second Peter 1:21 NKJV, we read: **For prophecy never came by the will of man, but holy men of God spoke as they were moved by the Holy Spirit.**

The Holy Spirit inspired men to write the Word of God, and that same divine inspiration is resident within the Word for those of us who read it and act on it today. Just as the Spirit of God moved on men to write the Scriptures, He will move on us as we act on or respond to those same eternal truths.

THE WORD: MORE THAN JUST INFORMATION

The power in God's Word is sufficient unto itself. In other words, it will stand on its own. Isaiah said that the Word of God will not return void, empty, or ineffective in any situation; rather, it will accomplish and prosper in what it was sent to do (Isaiah 55:11). The words "accomplish" and "prosper" indicate that the Word has the power to produce.

It could be easy to view the Word of God as mere information, but it is infinitely more than that. If the Word were only designed to inform, we would not be able to expect anything to happen when we preached it to others.

So many believers today are satisfied when the Word

they minister to others is released with anointing and true revelation. They forget, however, that the Word is anointed for one purpose: to produce a demonstration of that Word in the lives of those who hear it. Unless believers expect the Word to produce results, they will end up adhering to religious beliefs void of power (2 Timothy 3:5).

It is a deceptive trap to view the Word as information only. Consider the ministry of Jesus. We can see that as He preached, He knew His words were inspired, living containers of truth, not just information. In fact, He believed that the Holy Spirit and the life of God actually resided in His words. As a result, Jesus's words had a life-changing effect on the spirits and bodies of all who heard and received His words by faith.

David also grasped this truth. In Psalm 119:154, he prayed to God, **Quicken me according to thy word.** David understood that the Word has the power to quicken, to make alive, and to perform what it says.

THE POWER IN THE WORDS OF GOD

Consider the words of the apostle Paul in Hebrews 4:12 TLB:

> **For whatever God says to us is full of living power: it is sharper than the sharpest dagger, cut-**

ting swift and deep into our innermost thoughts and desires with all their parts, exposing us for what we really are.

When we are taught certain truths or ideas in a particular way, those beliefs become commonplace for us, whether they are correct or not. We become conditioned to accept them.

For example, many people are accustomed to hearing the Word of God preached, yet rarely do they see it demonstrated. Thus, they do not have the same degree of expectancy for results as those do who have seen the Word preached "with signs following." The way these people receive and respond to the Word has become conditioned by the presentation familiar to them.

Over the years I have observed that the way a person is brought into a relationship with God will be the benchmark for that individual's future experience. If that person sits under teaching that mixes the Word with traditional or religious ideas, those man-made doctrines will prove to be a hindrance in his walk with God.

Christians often struggle in their spiritual walks for years, bound by wrong concepts concerning God and His desire and willingness to bless them. That is why God said, **My people are destroyed for lack of knowledge** (Hosea 4:6). Since the lack of knowledge of God's will and His character brings destruction, it follows that the knowledge of His Word and His will produces life.

Hearing the gospel is certainly the first step toward knowing the truth and walking in God's best. However, the second step is also vitally important: seeing the power of the gospel demonstrated through the lives of others.

The apostle Paul addressed this second step when he admonished the Thessalonian Christians:

> **For this reason we also thank God without ceasing, because when you received the word of God which you heard from us, you welcomed it not as the word of men, but as it is in truth, the word of God, which also effectively works in you who believe.**
>
> **1 Thessalonians 2:13** NKJV

Paul stated that the Word of God received correctly will work effectively. In the original Greek language it means, "The Word will put forth a display of power."

If we as believers are hearing the wonderful news of God's goodness and then seeing the results that follow those words of life, our concept of the Word of God will be healthy. Remember, Jesus said that God wants us to be healthy branches, continually producing fruit as we stay vitally connected to the Vine, Jesus Christ (John 15:1-8).

Jesus Himself called attention to the fruit or the works of His ministry. For instance, when the disciples of John the Baptist asked Him if He was the Christ, Jesus told them to go tell John what they had heard and seen (See Matthew 11:3).

Would there have been great interest in the teaching ministry of Jesus if He had failed to produce results on a regular basis? Would multitudes have followed Him amidst so much opposition from the Pharisees and Sadducees and their doctrines if Jesus had preached just another powerless doctrine? I don't think so!

People were the same then as they are today—they want results. And Jesus preached a message that consistently produced results.

Luke 4:16-19 NKJV gives us insight into the message that Jesus preached everywhere He went:

> **So He came to Nazareth, where He had been brought up. And as His custom was, He went into the synagogue on the Sabbath day, and stood up to read.**
>
> **And He was handed the book of the prophet Isaiah. And when He had opened the book, He found the place where it was written:**
>
> **"The Spirit of the LORD is upon Me, because He has anointed Me to preach the gospel to the poor; He has sent Me to heal the brokenhearted, to proclaim liberty to the captives and recovery of sight to the blind, to set at liberty those who are oppressed;**

"To proclaim the acceptable year of the LORD."

As you can see, Jesus boldly declared to people that He was the fulfillment of the Prophet Isaiah's words. He did this not just to inform the people, but to produce results in their lives by the power resident within the words He spoke.

Notice how often Jesus produced results simply by the words He spoke. He spoke to the fig tree, and immediately it dried up from the roots (Matthew 21:18-19). He spoke to the winds and the waves, and immediately the storm ceased (Matthew 8:23-27). Jesus spoke the Word of healing to the centurion about his servant (Matthew 8:5-13), the nobleman's son (John 4:46-54), the blind man (John 9:1-7), the man with the withered hand (Matthew 12:9-13), and every one of them was healed. But most importantly, Jesus spoke of His victory over death, and the power of those words later raised Him out of the grave (John 10:17-18).

In Proverbs 18:21, Solomon wrote that the power of life and death is in the tongue. Therefore, in order for us to expect God to perform miracles through our words, we must first believe that our message is full of power. Then we must preach and teach the Word so the Holy Ghost can confirm our message (which is *His* message) "with signs following."

RESULTS FROM THE WORD

Is it any wonder that Jesus produced the results that He did? He knew ahead of time that results would follow if He obeyed only the words of eternal life. This knowledge produced an added confidence in Jesus that was recognizable, as we see in Mark 1:21-22:

> **And they went into Capernaum; and straightway on the sabbath day he entered into the synagogue, and taught.**
> **And they were astonished at his doctrine: for he taught them as one that had authority, and not as the scribes.**

Jesus preached with a confident attitude. He *expected* success. He didn't comprehend or consider even the possibility of failure.

Jesus also knew no fear. He was not intimidated by anyone. He knew the power of His Father's words; therefore, He had no reason to believe that what He said would not come to pass. He didn't attempt to prophesy something into being. *Instead, He spoke into existence on earth what was already a reality in heaven.* Jesus simply trusted and relied on the Holy Spirit to perform the words He spoke.

Can you imagine living your life the way Jesus did,

knowing that the words you speak will always be accomplished? This is the life God has called us to live, for in Jeremiah 1:12, He gives us this promise: **I will hasten my word to perform it.**

Then in Isaiah 55:8-11 NKJV, God makes this truth even clearer:

> **"For My thoughts are not your thoughts, nor are your ways My ways," says the LORD.**
>
> **"For as the heavens are higher than the earth, so are My ways higher than your ways, and My thoughts than your thoughts.**
>
> **"For as the rain comes down, and the snow from heaven, and do not return there, but water the earth, and make it bring forth and bud, that it may give seed to the sower and bread to the eater,**
>
> **"So shall My word be that goes forth from My mouth; it shall not return to Me void, but it shall accomplish what I please, and it shall prosper in the thing for which I sent it."**

Jesus understood very well what He was doing; He knew that His words would produce results. That is why He could speak with such authority.

For instance, when Jesus declared in John 10:30 that He was one with the Father, the Pharisees took up rocks to stone Him. Jesus asked them, "For which of these [good] works do you stone Me?" (v. 32 NKJV).

The Pharisees replied, "For a good work we do not stone You, but for blasphemy, and because You being a Man, make Yourself God." (v. 33).

Later Jesus said in verses 37 and 38:

"If I do not do the works of My Father, do not believe Me;

"But if I do, though you do not believe Me, believe the works, that you may know and believe that the Father is in Me, and I in Him."

Jesus was the Son of God, yet He understood that He also had to produce the *results* of the Son of God.

STEPPING OUT ON THE WATER

The more I allow the Holy Spirit to teach me along this line, the more I experience the truth that the Word alone will produce results. That's why I love taking the limits off God and like Peter, step out into the unknown with nothing but His Word and my faith beneath me.

Miracles are not in the boat. You have to get out of the boat to walk on the water.

I experienced stepping out of my comfort zone early

one spring. I was preparing for my regular schedule of meetings. For a moment I thought about an upcoming youth meeting that was scheduled for the summer. More than one church and a few hundred youth would be participating in the meeting.

I am not used to conducting youth meetings and, to be honest, I was nervous about this particular meeting. So I began talking to the Lord about it. I told Him I wanted to capture the young people's attention right away so the ministry of the Word would be easier.

Suddenly, like a flash before my eyes, I saw myself do something in that youth meeting. It was so quick that it was difficult for me to tell whether I actually saw it or just knew it in my spirit. In that sudden flash, I saw myself challenge the strongest guy in the room to an arm-wrestling match. I told the young people that if I couldn't easily defeat him, they wouldn't have to believe a thing I told them during the rest of the camp.

Over the next few months as I pondered the thought of actually doing this, I experienced mixed emotions. At times, I'd be inspired by the thought and get rather excited. At other times, I'd begin to reason myself out of it.

But I have learned that in order for us to see the miraculous, we have to commit ourselves to stepping out of our comfort zone. So one evening when some friends came over to the house, I told them what I planned to do in the upcoming youth service. One person made the comment that he knew of others who had said and done such things in services and had ruined their ministries because things didn't quite work out the way they had anticipated.

However, I have been working with God like this for years now, and I am still in the ministry. I know that God wants to back me up when I step out in faith, just as He wants to back up every one of His children. So I said, "I am willing to risk making a mistake if there is any chance I might get it right."

A great man of God once said to me, "Stepping out to do what you believe God is saying for you to do will cause you to learn one way or another. If you are right, you will learn to follow the leading of the Lord. If you are wrong, at least you will learn which way not to do it again. Those who never step out will never learn either way. They will miss it because they didn't step out, and they will never learn whether or not they were correct." This man's words proved to be good advice over the years, and his counsel served me well in this instance.

When the time came to go to the youth meeting, I was still tossing around the idea of whether or not I should try what I had seen myself doing. It seemed so difficult to make up my mind. In the end, that was the very reason I decided to step out in faith and try it.

I found the strongest guy in the youth meeting and then told everyone what was going to happen. I didn't say

I was about to *attempt* to do something; I told them what I was *going* to do.

You see, if we leave room for error, to accommodate the possibility of failure, the Word will never work for us. We must operate in the same bold authority with which Jesus taught. Remember, previously I asked the Lord for assistance in capturing the attention of the youth who would attend that meeting. The Spirit of God gave me that illustration as His answer. It is important to note that you can only expect God to back you up if you have His written Word as the basis for your action or if you have the leading of His voice as the source of your direction.

As I encouraged the young man to come forward, you can imagine the stir it created with the young people. They especially got interested when I emphatically declared more than once that if what I was about to do didn't work, either I would leave or they wouldn't have to believe another word I said. After all, I hadn't even begun to teach yet!

The young man got out of his seat and came forward. I could tell he was under the influence of the Holy Ghost. I had been counting on that! When the youth reached the front, he turned to face me. As he took my hand, I was conscious of the life of God flowing out of me, and I knew I had him beat.

Before we started the match, I stopped for a moment and talked to the young people about the law of contact and transmission. I explained that the contact of my hands transmits the power of God to the one I am touching.

Then I asked the associate pastor to referee the match. But when he touched our hands to start the match, the power of God caused him to fall in a heap on my opponent! I told the associate pastor in jest that I didn't need his help; then the young man and I began the arm-wrestling contest.

The match was over very quickly. It wasn't difficult for me to win, but it was the work of the Holy Ghost that made all the difference.

MINISTERING THE WORD BY THE SPIRIT OF FAITH

All this happened at that youth meeting because of the power of words. I didn't say the power of *suggestion*; it was the power of God released through *words*.

I will give you another illustration. Not long ago at a ministers' meeting, I took the opportunity to experiment with this principle even further. I wanted to rely on the power of the gospel alone without any help from the method of my delivery. Therefore, the text I chose was Romans 6:1-2:

> **What shall we say then? Shall we continue in sin, that grace may abound? God forbid. How shall we, that are dead to sin, live any longer therein?**

Everywhere this scripture uses the word "sin," I replaced it with the word "sickness," since both of these words originate from the same root word. Then I asked the question, "What shall we say? Shall we continue to be sick that grace may abound? God forbid!"

Most of those attending the meeting were ministers. As I preached on the sixth chapter of Romans, I continued to remind them that the Word preached will bring results. And that is exactly what happened. We had some of the most wonderful results in that meeting, and most of them took place without the laying on of hands.

For instance, a woman with a large growth in her breast was completely healed. A man who had suffered forty years with a damaged knee was healed. God also healed a woman with arthritis in her hips and knees.

A man with poor eyesight was healed so that he could read perfectly without glasses. Another man was healed of high blood pressure. God also healed a woman of chronic trouble in her hip joint. This woman was a physical therapist by profession, and she later related that she hadn't been able to even cross her legs because of the pain. But Jesus healed her. All this happened because I believed that the Word would produce results as it was preached, just as it did with Jesus.

The ministry of Jesus did not consist of just teaching and preaching, as we have seen so often in the church today. Jesus always taught with a complete mastery of the subject. The dominion and authority in His words arose from the absoluteness of God's truth and Jesus's certainty of its results. Jesus taught with a spirit of faith and the confidence of knowing that what He said would come to pass.

I have heard prophets say that in these last days, we will see an increase of the spirit of seeing and knowing. I believe that part of the increase of knowing will be demonstrated as we teach and preach with such confidence in the results before we see them that we transmit to the people the spirit of faith, or the God-kind of belief.

We must contend for proper esteem of the Word of God and for the Word to be respected and taught with faith. Only when we respect the Word of God as the very life and power of God will we experience the transmission of spiritual life substance into a physical being.

That is what transpired each time Jesus taught or preached. That is what *we* must have as well if signs are to follow our ministry of the Word.

Chapter 2

THE HEALING MINISTRY OF JESUS

The gospels are full of accounts of divine healing through the ministry of Jesus. Most of these healings occurred in the setting of multitudes being healed.

The Scriptures mention nineteen individual cases of divine healing in the life of Jesus, all of which are significant to understanding the way Jesus ministered.

THE "MAN SIDE" VS. THE "GOD SIDE" OF BLESSING

First and foremost, it is important to realize that Jesus spent much of His time ministering the Word to His disciples and to the multitudes. As we know, Jesus is the Incarnate Word Himself; therefore, the standard for His ministry—while He walked on the earth and now through us—is the Word of God.

One of the primary reasons Jesus ministered the Word was to build faith in the hearts of those who listened. He knew that one effective method for receiving divine healing is through the faith of the individual who has been taught the Word. We could call this the "man side" of healing.

This method is actually the most preferred because it produces the most lasting results. The emphasis of this method of healing is on the individual's responsibility to hear the Word of God, whether from someone else or through personal study, and then to act on the Word to receive his healing. Thus, with the "man side" method of healing, the responsibility rests on the individual himself to hear, act on, and receive the desired results.

Conversely, the "God side" of healing refers to the times that God initiates His will through someone on behalf of another for the good of all. In this case, God usually works through a person who is sensitive and responsive to Him so that the recipient will be blessed. In this instance, we have an example of the gifts of the Spirit in operation. As mentioned in First Corinthians 12, any gift of the Spirit is an endowment of power that produces results.

In Mark 4:1-20, Jesus made reference to the power of

the Word to produce results when it is truly received and acted on by those who hear it:

> And he began again to teach by the sea side: and there was gathered unto him a great multitude, so that he entered into a ship, and sat in the sea; and the whole multitude was by the sea on the land.
>
> And he taught them many things by parables, and said unto them in his doctrine,
>
> Hearken; Behold, there went out a sower to sow:
>
> And it came to pass, as he sowed, some fell by the way side, and the fowls of the air came and devoured it up.
>
> And some fell on stony ground, where it had not much earth; and immediately it sprang up, because it had no depth of earth:
>
> But when the sun was up, it was scorched; and because it had no root, it withered away.
>
> And some fell among thorns, and the thorns grew up, and choked it, and it yielded no fruit.
>
> And other fell on good ground, and did yield fruit that sprang up and increased; and brought forth, some thirty, and some sixty, and some an hundred.

And he said unto them, He that hath ears to hear, let him hear.

And when he was alone, they that were about him with the twelve asked of him the parable.

And he said unto them, Unto you it is given to know the mystery of the kingdom of God: but unto them that are without, all these things are done in parables:

That seeing they may see, and not perceive; and hearing they may hear, and not understand; lest at any time they should be converted, and their sins should be forgiven them.

And he said unto them, Know ye not this parable? and how then will ye know all parables?

The sower soweth the word.

And these are they by the way side, where the word is sown; but when they have heard, Satan cometh immediately, and taketh away the word that was sown in their hearts.

And these are they likewise which are sown on stony ground; who, when they have heard the word, immediately receive it with gladness;

And have no root in themselves, and so endure but for a time: afterward, when affliction or persecution ariseth for the word's sake, immediately they are offended.

**And these are they which are sown among
thorns; such as hear the word,**

**And the cares of this world, and the deceitful-
ness of riches, and the lusts of other things entering
in, choke the word, and it becometh unfruitful.**

**And these are they which are sown on good
ground; such as hear the word, and receive it, and
bring forth fruit, some thirtyfold, some sixty, and
some an hundred.**

As Jesus explained in this passage of scripture, the seed
that is sown is the Word that is preached. So the emphasis
in this parable is on the ministry of the Word of God.

In this parable we see four different kinds of soil. The
only soil that produced and maintained the desired results
was the good soil, which represents the hearer who receives
and acts on the Word.

Jesus spoke of this same principle in Matthew 7:24-27
when He related a parable about two builders. The first
builder was wise, for he built his house on the rocks.
When the wind and the storm came, the house was left
standing because of its sturdy foundation. This wise
builder represents the person who hears the Word and
then acts on the Word he hears.

Conversely, the foolish builder built his house on the
sand. When the storm came, the house fell because it had

no foundation. This second builder represents the person who hears the Word but doesn't act on it.

As believers in this modern day, we have much to be thankful for. We have been living in such a tremendous era, during which the Word of God has had great prominence in our local churches.

Back in Martin Luther's day, the Word of God was locked up for the clergy only, and the common man was kept ignorant of the truth. The spiritual and intellectual darkness was so prevalent during that time period that it is still referred to as the Dark Ages.

Thank God, we are encouraged to study and embrace the Word today. Yet we must also recognize that we will only receive its benefits as we determine not only to hear the Word, but to act on it as well.

To consider the results of the good soil in Jesus's parable of the sower, we must first tally up the harvest. Suppose all four types of soil represented 100 people. In that case, the good soil would represent 25 of those 100 people. When the Word was preached, one-third of those 25 people received 30-percent results, one-third received 60-percent results, and one-third received 100-percent results. Thus, when we do the math, we find that only about eight people received 100 percent complete results from the Word that was preached.

This outcome doesn't sound very good when we put it this way. Why did Jesus's ministry have better results? How can we reach the other 75 people who aren't having results? I believe the Bible provides the answers to these questions, which we will explore later.

EXAMPLES OF THE MAN SIDE OF HEALING

Now consider the two individual cases that represent the "man side" method of healing. The best case study is found in Mark 5:25-34:

> And a certain woman, which had an issue of blood twelve years,
>
> And had suffered many things of many physicians, and had spent all that she had, and was nothing bettered, but rather grew worse,
>
> When she had heard of Jesus, came in the press behind, and touched his garment.
>
> For she said, If I may touch but his clothes, I shall be whole.
>
> And straightway the fountain of her blood was dried up; and she felt in her body that she was healed of that plague.
>
> And Jesus, immediately knowing in himself that virtue had gone out of him, turned him about in the press, and said, Who touched my clothes?

And his disciples said unto him, Thou seest the multitude thronging thee, and sayest thou, Who touched me?

And he looked round about to see her that had done this thing.

But the woman fearing and trembling, knowing what was done in her, came and fell down before him, and told him all the truth.

And he said unto her, Daughter, thy faith hath made thee whole; go in peace, and be whole of thy plague.

It is easy to see how this healing falls into the "man side" category. This woman was desperate for help. When she heard the message about Jesus, she determined to act on her newfound belief. There is no record that anyone else was involved in her decision except perhaps those who may have conveyed the message to her.

The woman said to herself, "If I can touch the hem of His garment, I will be well." Then she made her way to Jesus as He was passing through the crowd. When she finally drew near to Him, she reached out and touched Him, just as she had determined to do. At that very moment, the disease left her. It is at this time that we see Jesus's involvement in the healing.

Of course, Jesus is and always will be the focus of all healing. Yet as we view this case from afar, we can see why the woman was already healed before Jesus entered the situation. The woman was healed because of her action of faith. She heard, she believed, she acted, and she received—a perfect example of a "man side" healing.

Most sermons that are preached on this subject focus on this type of healing. The preacher presents his message, expecting the people to hear and receive. Then he encourages the people to hold on to what they believe they have received.

Yet as we have seen, if it is possible that only eight out of a hundred people will actually receive the desired results from the teaching of the Word in this manner, there must be some way of improving the number of needs that are met when the Word is sown into people's hearts. *Jesus was and is the answer for every person's problems.*

The second example that can be included in this "man side" category is found in Matthew 8:5-10:

> **And when Jesus was entered into Capernaum, there came unto him a centurion, beseeching him,**
>
> **And saying, Lord, my servant lieth at home sick of the palsy, grievously tormented.**
>
> **And Jesus saith unto him, I will come and heal him.**
>
> **The centurion answered and said, Lord, I am not worthy that thou shouldest come under my**

roof: but speak the word only, and my servant
shall be healed.

For I am a man under authority, having sol-
diers under me: and I say to this man, Go, and he
goeth; and to another, Come, and he cometh; and
to my servant, Do this, and he doeth it.

When Jesus heard it, he marvelled, and said to
them that followed, Verily I say unto you, I have
not found so great faith, no, not in Israel.

Notice that in this situation, the centurion already
knew what he believed and what was necessary for the
desired healing to come to pass. He didn't need any help;
he believed that one word from Jesus would heal his servant. The centurion therefore related his conviction and
the results he expected to the proper authority—in this
case, Jesus. This Gentile man understood that just as the
authority delegated to him caused servants to obey when
he gave the command, the same principle would be in
operation if Jesus spoke the Word concerning his servant's
healing.

Look at Jesus's response to the faith demonstrated by
the centurion:

And I say unto you, That many shall come
from the east and west, and shall sit down with

Abraham, and Isaac, and Jacob, in the kingdom of heaven.

But the children of the kingdom shall be cast out into outer darkness: there shall be weeping and gnashing of teeth.

And Jesus said unto the centurion, Go thy way; and as thou hast believed, so be it done unto thee. And his servant was healed in the selfsame hour.

Matthew 8:11-13

Again, we see someone who heard truth, believed what he heard, and acted on it with conviction. It is interesting to note that Jesus would have gone to the centurion's home to heal his servant if necessary. However, because of this man's faith, one word from the Master was sufficient to produce the servant's healing.

You can see why the man side, or the faith side, is the most desired method of receiving healing. When this method is in operation, the strong convictions of the people requesting healing produce results, as does their equally strong resolve to hold on to their healing once it is received.

The knowledge and the faith of the two individuals in these examples are to be commended. It would be wonderful if preaching alone would produce these kinds of results every time.

Unfortunately, this is not true in the modern-day church. The preaching and teaching of the Word has not come close to meeting the needs of the people the way God intends.

One reason for this is that Jesus didn't teach the Word the way we do today. He included an ingredient that is missing in most modern-day teaching of the Word. This missing ingredient is the focal point of this book and my primary reason for writing it. Only when it is added to our teaching and preaching of the Word will we see multitudes desiring to touch the hem of Jesus's garment, as did the woman with the issue of blood.

THE GOD SIDE OF HEALING: GIVEN AS THE SPIRIT WILLS

As we continue to study Jesus's ministry, we will see that there are other ways to minister healing to people as well. As I mentioned earlier, there is the "God side" method of healing.

God has reserved the right to manifest Himself through the work of the Holy Ghost. Paul wrote about these manifestations in First Corinthians 12:7-11 NKJV:

> **But the manifestation of the Spirit is given to each one for the profit of all:**

for to one is given the word of wisdom through the Spirit, to another the word of knowledge through the same Spirit,

to another faith by the same Spirit, to another gifts of healings by the same Spirit,

to another the working of miracles, to another prophecy, to another discerning of spirits, to another different kinds of tongues, to another the interpretation of tongues.

But one and the same Spirit works all these things, distributing to each one individually as He wills.

The last phrase in verse 11 says that these manifestations are given *as the Spirit of God wills*. In other words, God will move at various times to increase the effectiveness of His plan. The nine ways mentioned in the passage above are the common ways He moves from His side toward man.

From one perspective, God has already moved toward us through the finished work of Christ. We have nothing to wait for concerning salvation and everything it encompasses; rather, our redemption is available according to our action of faith toward God.

Yet God in His goodness still continues to initiate blessing toward man through the work of the Holy Ghost. With this premise in mind, consider the following examples from the ministry of Jesus.

One case in particular stands out as a definite "God side" case of healing. It is found in John 5:1-9 NKJV:

> After this there was a feast of the Jews, and Jesus went up to Jerusalem.
>
> Now there is in Jerusalem by the Sheep Gate a pool, which is called in Hebrew, Bethesda, having five porches.
>
> In these lay a great multitude of sick people, blind, lame, paralyzed, waiting for the moving of the water.
>
> For an angel went down at a certain time into the pool and stirred up the water; then whoever stepped in first, after the stirring of the water, was made well of whatever disease he had.
>
> Now a certain man was there who had an infirmity thirty-eight years.
>
> When Jesus saw him lying there, and knew that he already had been in that condition a long time, He said to him, "Do you want to be made well?"
>
> The sick man answered Him, "Sir, I have no man to put me into the pool when the water is stirred up; but while I am coming, another steps down before me."
>
> Jesus said to him, "Rise, take up your bed and walk."

And immediately the man was made well, took up his bed, and walked. And that day was the Sabbath.

We know that this man had no faith working toward Jesus because he had no knowledge of who Jesus was. When later questioned about who had made him well, he was unable to provide an answer (John 5:10-13). Already we can see that this is very different from the "man side" method of healing.

Notice that when Jesus approached this man and asked him if he wanted to be made well, the man replied that he didn't have anyone to put him into the water when it was stirred. This paralyzed man was completely oblivious to who Jesus was. He never asked Jesus why He would inquire about his condition, nor did he seem to care.

However, when Jesus told the man to rise and walk, the man obviously realized that his legs had become whole. Once he knew his healing had come, he immediately responded to Jesus's command.

You can see by this example that the man used no faith in Jesus to initiate the healing. Anyone can walk when his legs are strong and healthy.

Jesus said to doubting Thomas (my paraphrase), "You believe because you see Me; anyone can do this. It takes a person of faith to believe before he sees any results." (See John 20:29.)

The results of these two methods of ministry are the same, yet the operation of these two approaches is very different indeed.

You will find that most people trust more in this latter approach to divine healing than any other. Like the man at the Pool of Bethesda, they are waiting either for someone or something divine to happen before they will believe anything.

Whether this man was the recipient of a gift of special faith or a gift of healing because of God's initiation through Jesus, one thing is clear: The man would still be lying there if God hadn't supernaturally moved on his behalf. As you can see, this case represents the God side of healing very well.

In the next chapter, we will assign each case to a side only after we have discussed the possibility of a third side. If there were only two sides, the standard approach would be to list twelve cases on the man side or the faith side and seven on the God side or the gift side.

The reason this listing is acceptable is that twelve of the healing accounts either mention faith or imply that faith was used; the others would therefore automatically fall on the gift side. If there are only two sides, this equation would be logical; however, if a third side exists, the equation would have to be changed.

LACK OF RESULTS NOT GOD'S FAULT

Let me remind you again that we are discussing the ministry of Jesus. If we are accurate in our assumptions about divine healing, we should have the results to prove them in our own lives and ministry, just as Jesus did when He walked on this earth. He placed the validation of His ministry on the works He performed, as He noted in John 10:37 NKJV: **If I do not do the works of My Father, do not believe Me.**

The church at large has done the opposite. Many Christians don't want to be responsible for their own inadequacy, so they blame their lack of results on God and try to act as spiritual as possible. This is the reason the doctrine of divine healing has evolved the way it has. But how much more could the kingdom of God be furthered if Christians began to accept responsibility for their results or their lack of results?

In the denomination I grew up in, I remember we always attributed all problems to the sovereignty of God. Simply put, our way of thinking was as follows: "God is allowing this problem, so we will give Him praise for strength to get through it."

That is no different from the way many modern-day Charismatic or Pentecostal tongue-talkers think. They are waiting for the "last-day move" so the church can rise up and become the church God has called her to be. In essence, this way of thinking wrongly concludes that it is God's fault that Christians are so ill-equipped and under-privileged.

This discussion is far from over, however. We have much more Word to explore as we seek to understand how to fulfill Jesus's command to do the same works He did—and even greater—until He comes.

Chapter 3

GOD HAS ALWAYS NEEDED A MEDIATOR

The man-side and the God-side approaches to the ministry of Jesus may seem to fit our own experience of ministering to others, but they are not the only approaches that fit *Jesus's* ministry. Remember, we still haven't answered the question, "Why did Jesus have better results than we do?"

Traditionally, we would say, "He had better results because He was Jesus!" However, the disciples also produced great results, just as Jesus did. In fact, all through the centuries there have been those who have defied the norm and stepped out in God.

Do these events take place in response to a sovereign move of God? Does everything revolve around God's timetable as though He were controlling the results that are destined for only a few? If that is true, we need to tell Aunt Bessie, "When the move of God gets here, we will be able to help you, but for right now, you just have to hold on."

WHY CHRISTIANS DON'T MEASURE UP TO JESUS'S MINISTRY

Ephesians 4:18 NKJV is a Scripture that will help us at this juncture.Paul describes the unbeliving Gentiles as:

> **Having their understanding darkened, being alienated from the life of God, because of the ignorance that is in them, because of the blindness of their heart.** The New International Version says, **Due to the hardening of their hearts.**

As this Scripture states, ignorance and hardness of heart alienate people or make them nonparticipants in the life of God. This is a tragedy. If there is anything we should want working for us, it is the life of God. This is what made the difference in the life and ministry of Jesus. The life of God is also what you and I received when we were born again.

Notice the seriousness of ignorance and hardness of heart. When people don't know God's truth, or when they know it but are unwilling to cooperate with it, they forfeit their rights and privileges to access or appropriate the power of God's life.

Yes, there is a tremendous supply of God's Spirit that is available to the body of Christ in this hour. But there are two main reasons Christians don't measure up to the ministry of Jesus: (1) they are stuck in a theological rut and don't want to experience more of God at the expense of staying complacent and prideful, or (2) they lack knowledge and don't understand the spiritual equipment that is available to them to utilize so they can enjoy God's highest in this life.

I don't know about you, but I don't want to miss the divine blessings that are right in front of me just because I am not willing to challenge what I think I know or what I have been taught. If the results of my life and ministry don't measure up to the life and ministry of Jesus, I want God to show me the necessary steps I need to take to obtain what I am missing.

THE ROLE OF THOSE WHO "STAND IN THE GAP"

As stated earlier, the Bible gives nineteen individual cases of divine healing in the ministry of Jesus. We have discussed three of those cases, but what about the other sixteen examples of healing in the Gospels?

Let's explore the reason why there are sixteen individual

cases of healing in Jesus's ministry that don't seem to easily fit in either of the two categories that we have discussed so far.

First Timothy 2:5 NKJV says, **For there is one God and one Mediator between God and men, the Man Christ Jesus.** Here we see that the man side and the God side are both valid methods for blessing. But sandwiched in between these two sides is the need for a mediator. Even in the Old Testament, there was always a need for someone to "stand in the gap" for the people.

For instance, Psalm 106:23 refers to a time when Moses stood as Israel's mediator before God:

> **Therefore he said that he would destroy them, had not Moses his chosen stood before him in the breach, to turn away his wrath, lest he should destroy them.**

This scenario is related in Numbers 14:11-20:

> **And the LORD said unto Moses, How long will this people provoke me? and how long will it be ere they believe me, for all the signs which I have shewed among them?**
>
> **I will smite them with the pestilence, and disinherit them, and will make of thee a greater nation and mightier than they.**

And Moses said unto the LORD, Then the Egyptians shall hear it, (for thou broughtest up this people in thy might from among them;)

And they will tell it to the inhabitants of this land: for they have heard that thou LORD art among this people, that thou LORD art seen face to face, and that thy cloud standeth over them, and that thou goest before them, by day time in a pillar of a cloud, and in a pillar of fire by night.

Now if thou shalt kill all this people as one man, then the nations which have heard the fame of thee will speak, saying,

Because the LORD was not able to bring this people into the land which he sware unto them, therefore he hath slain them in the wilderness.

And now, I beseech thee, let the power of my Lord be great, according as thou hast spoken, saying,

The LORD is longsuffering, and of great mercy, forgiving iniquity and transgression, and by no means clearing the guilty, visiting the iniquity of the fathers upon the children unto the third and fourth generation.

Pardon, I beseech thee, the iniquity of this people according unto the greatness of thy mercy, and as thou hast forgiven this people, from Egypt even until now.

And the LORD said, I have pardoned according to thy word.

Ezekiel also speaks of the Lord's desire to find a mediator so He can move on behalf of His people:

> **And I sought for a man among them, that should make up the hedge, and stand in the gap before me for the land, that I should not destroy it: but I found none.**
>
> **Therefore have I poured out mine indignation upon them; I have consumed them with the fire of my wrath: their own way have I recompensed upon their heads, saith the Lord GOD.**
>
> **Ezekiel 22:30-31**

This is a serious matter, for the lack of mediators who are willing to stand in the gap for others can have such an adverse effect on so many lives.

In the book of Judges, we see that whenever the children of Israel needed to be saved from their enemies, the Lord would raise up a deliverer. The same pattern persisted time and time again. All would go well for the nation as long as the people were serving the Lord. But during the course of time, the people would become rebellious and self-sufficient and start living a lifestyle of sin. This would eventually spiral them into negative situations, such as sickness or trouble with other nations.

In their distress, the people would cry out to the Lord for help. God would hear their cry and send someone as His representative to deliver them and turn them to the Lord.

This pattern sounds all too familiar, doesn't it?

JESUS, THE MASTER MEDIATOR

Every deliverer and mediator in the Old Testament served as a type and shadow of the Lord Jesus Christ. And if Jesus remains the standard for all who have ever delivered or stood in the gap for others, then we as the body of Christ must understand His ministry and purpose.

When Jesus came into the earth as a babe, His name—Emmanuel—represented the fact that God was with us (Matthew 1:23). Looking at the life of Jesus, we can see that this means more than just His presence making everything happen. Jesus came with a specific purpose: to destroy the works of the devil (1 John 3:8). He was anointed to do a specific task. This task is described in Acts 10:38, which sums up the earthly ministry of Jesus:

God anointed Jesus of Nazareth with the Holy Ghost and with power: who went about doing

good, and healing all that were oppressed of the devil; for God was with him.

So what are *we* doing in our own lives and ministries to follow Jesus's example? Most of us at best are either waiting for the people to respond to the Word and receive, or we are waiting for a move of the Holy Ghost to initiate a miracle. Both positions involve waiting, which is something Jesus did not do.

CONNECTING MAN WITH THE FATHER GOD

As we continue to consider the healing ministry of Jesus, we will first look at Luke 5:17-25:

> And it came to pass on a certain day, as he was teaching, that there were Pharisees and doctors of the law sitting by, which were come out of every town of Galilee, and Judaea, and Jerusalem: and the power of the Lord was present to heal them.
> And, behold, men brought in a bed a man which was taken with a palsy: and they sought means to bring him in, and to lay him before him.
> And when they could not find by what way they might bring him in because of the multitude, they went upon the housetop, and let him down

through the tiling with his couch into the midst before Jesus.

And when he saw their faith, he said unto him, Man, thy sins are forgiven thee.

And the scribes and the Pharisees began to reason, saying, Who is this which speaketh blasphemies? Who can forgive sins, but God alone?

But when Jesus perceived their thoughts, he answering said unto them, What reason ye in your hearts?

Whether is easier, to say, Thy sins be forgiven thee; or to say, Rise up and walk?

But that ye may know that the Son of man hath power upon earth to forgive sins, (he said unto the sick of the palsy,) I say unto thee, Arise, and take up thy couch, and go into thine house.

And immediately he rose up before them, and took up that whereon he lay, and departed to his own house, glorifying God.

In this passage, we find that Jesus was teaching in a house filled with inquisitive Pharisees and teachers of the Law. Verse 17 tells us that the power of the Lord was present to heal all. This reveals the great mercy of God. It was His intention to heal every person in that place.

Although only one man was healed, verse 20 seems to indicate that this is an instance of a man-initiated healing because the man who was healed had faith. But the question must be asked, "Where did this man's faith begin and end?" In other words, "Just what did this man believe?"

Verse 18 says, **They** [the paralytic man and his four friends] **sought means to bring him in.** This statement declares what the five men believed. They all believed that Jesus was the answer. They believed that if they could get to Jesus, the sick man would be healed.

In this passage, the word "sought" reveals *intention.* These men planned together to take this journey. The paralytic man was not going to let his friends take him just anywhere; he wanted to be taken to *Jesus.* And I am sure the four friends told him that this wasn't going to be a round trip ticket. They would carry him only one way because they fully expected the man to be healed once he was in the presence of Jesus.

The men's planning meeting was itself an expression of their faith. Their journey was their faith in action. When they encountered opposition at the house where Jesus was teaching, it was an opportunity to test whether they would fail or succeed in their intentions.

The men passed the test with flying colors. They were determined to accomplish what they set out to do—and they did. In verse 20, Jesus *saw* their faith. For that matter, so did everyone else.

Let's stop and analyze what actually happened in this story. The paralytic man and his friends definitely had the faith to get to Jesus. The extreme measures the four men took to place their friend in the presence of Jesus was the demonstration of their faith. Jesus and the others *saw* what these men believed and expected.

But if faith was present and the power was present, why was there no immediate healing?

Here's the reason: *even though a person is in the presence of God's power, his faith still has to be released in order for a connection to be made with that power.*

This man didn't know what to do to release his faith. Unless someone helped him, he might have continued to lie on that bed of sickness indefinitely.

As we study these sixteen individual cases, we will see that Jesus was a Master at moving people into the appropriate response of faith so they could receive their healing. This is exactly what He did here.

Jesus told this man his sins were forgiven (v. 20.) At this point, the question of whether this man or God initiated his healing no longer applied to this situation. The man, unlike the woman with the issue of blood, did not believe, receive, and walk in the blessing by himself. He believed to a certain extent, but Jesus had to help him the rest of the way.

Therefore, this case in the ministry of Jesus reveals another method of healing as presented in the Gospels. Because Jesus was involved in instructing and empowering this man's faith, we could call this method the "God-man side."

There is one mediator between the God side and the man side—the man Christ Jesus. How crucial is this fact in duplicating the ministry of Jesus? I believe it is one of the primary missing ingredients that has caused the lack of success in the ministry of healing within the body of Christ.

If we, like Pilate, are only interested in washing our hands of any responsibility for the lack of God's power demonstrated in our lives, we will never approach the effectiveness of our Mentor, Jesus. Nor will we ever produce results if we're always waiting to see if the Holy Spirit is going to initiate a gift of the Spirit while we preach or teach a noncommittal message that doesn't require people to respond in active faith.

Jesus shows us that there is a way we can help the recipient. Let's complete this case study before commenting further.

The man who was let down through the roof didn't know what to do next as he lay paralyzed before Jesus. Then Jesus gave him a command of faith, which was simply a word for the man to believe in and act upon. Jesus said to him, "Son, your sins are forgiven."

At that point, the man was released to get up and walk—*if* he had understood what Jesus was actually saying to him. The religious people in attendance hardened their hearts to the command of Jesus, which provoked the Master to confront their unbelief. He said to them, "Which is easier to say, 'Your sins be forgiven' or 'Rise up and walk'?" (See v. 23).

In reality, these two statements were saying the same thing. The One who possesses the divine authority to declare, "Your sins are forgiven," also possesses the divine power to cause a paralyzed man to rise up and walk!

The point I'm making here is that Jesus helped the man release his faith. We could say that *Jesus connected the God side and the man side together by assuming the position of a mediator.*

MINISTERS ARE CALLED TO BE MEDIATORS

For years, God's sheep have longed for shepherds to lead them into the miraculous. So many have needed help in releasing their faith, yet all they have received is more of the same powerless, ineffective rhetoric.

Here is a good illustration that might help you realize the necessity of "God-men"—men with the nature of God—champions in the earth. Suppose I were a shepherd who went out and scouted the land for good pastures and clear running water. Eventually I would find what I was looking for, but then my challenge would be to get the sheep to the new location. So I would gather all the sheep together and tell them about my find.

"There's an easy way to get there," I explain. "Just go up over the hill to the piney woods. Stay to the left of the forest until you reach a big boulder; then turn left and follow the ravine until you reach the pasture. Once you arrive at the pasture, go east until you run into the quiet stream about a quarter of a mile away."

Do you think the sheep will have a fighting chance of reaching the new location? If I were a betting man, I would wager that not one sheep will make it—and if one did make it, it would only be by accident.

What is the crucial ingredient needed for the sheep's success in this illustration? The shepherd. If the sheep are ever going to experience the blessings that await them in the new location, the shepherd will need to lead them there.

The same thing is true in the body of Christ. God considers the minister—the pastor or the undershepherd —responsible for leading the flock entrusted to his care to a place in the Spirit where the man side and the God side connect and God's blessings are thus received. Ezekiel 34:1-16 NKJV sheds some light on how God views this issue:

And the word of the LORD came to me, saying, "Son of man, prophesy against the shepherds of Israel, prophesy, and say to them, 'Thus says

the Lord GOD to the shepherds: "Woe to the shepherds of Israel who feed themselves! Should not the shepherds feed the flocks?

"You eat the fat and clothe yourselves with the wool; you slaughter the fatlings, but you do not feed the flock.

"The weak you have not strengthened, nor have you healed those who were sick, nor bound up the broken, nor brought back what was driven away, nor sought what was lost; but with force and cruelty you have ruled them.

"So they were scattered because there was no shepherd; and they became food for all the beasts of the field when they were scattered.

"My sheep wandered through all the mountains, and on every high hill; yes, My flock was scattered over the whole face of the earth, and no one was seeking or searching for them."

'Therefore, you shepherds, hear the word of the LORD:

"As I live," says the Lord GOD, "surely because My flock became a prey, and My flock became food for every beast of the field, because there was no shepherd, nor did My shepherds search for My flock, but the shepherds fed themselves and did not feed My flock"—

'therefore, O shepherds, hear the word of the LORD!

'Thus says the Lord GOD: "Behold, I am against the shepherds, and I will require My flock at their hand; I will cause them to cease feeding the sheep, and the shepherds shall feed themselves no more; for I will deliver My flock from their mouths, that they may no longer be food for them."

'For thus says the Lord GOD: "Indeed I Myself will search for My sheep and seek them out.

"As a shepherd seeks out his flock on the day he is among his scattered sheep, so will I seek out My sheep and deliver them from all the places where they were scattered on a cloudy and dark day.

"And I will bring them out from the peoples and gather them from the countries, and will bring them to their own land; I will feed them on the mountains of Israel, in the valleys and in all the inhabited places of the country.

"I will feed them in good pasture, and their fold shall be on the high mountains of Israel. There they shall lie down in a good fold and feed in rich pasture on the mountains of Israel.

"I will feed My flock, and I will make them lie down," says the Lord GOD.

"I will seek what was lost and bring back what was driven away, bind up the broken and

**strengthen what was sick; but I will destroy the fat
and the strong, and feed them in judgment."**

Can you see how serious it is to God that shepherds
follow the job description of the Great Shepherd? Jesus
Himself said that He is the Good Shepherd and that a
good shepherd takes care of his sheep (John 10:11). And
in these sixteen individual cases of divine healing, Jesus
also stood in the position of a mediator, who through His
wisdom, faith, anointing, and direction delivered and set
people free.

It is unjust for the preacher in the pulpit to blame
the people in the pews for their incompetence or lack of
fire. Of course, people do have a choice whether or not
they will receive the blessings of God. We can see this in
the ministry of Jesus in His own hometown. Because
the people there chose to take offense with Him, their
unbelief nullified their ability to receive God's power
(Matthew 13:53-58). However, most people are very
pliable when they receive help from ministers who are
committed to their success.

It should be noted here that the apostle Paul placed
great emphasis on the responsibility of all members of the
body of Christ to grow and develop in their faith. By no
means does this place blame on or direct criticism toward
the minister. Paul provided a balanced application of
responsibility for all members of the body of Christ to
achieve growth and development.

Ministers are gifts to the body of Christ who have been called to provide both anointed teaching and demonstrations of God's power as a package to the people. This then helps the listeners receive the message of the gospel by faith and produce results for God's kingdom in their own lives.

Yet there is so much lack of effort in the body of Christ in this regard, and it usually has to do with wrong thinking. Too often ministers leave the impression in the minds of their hearers that whatever the people lack will be supplied through a mighty move of God.

This misunderstanding only encourages people to accept their inadequacies rather than to overcome them. According to this mind-set, everything they can or cannot do becomes dependent on and proportionate to the extent of the move they have in their church.

A startling reality we must comprehend, however, is that the day Jesus moved into our hearts, we actually *became* "a move." When we move, so does God.

THE GOD-MAN CONNECTION IN BARTIMAEUS'S HEALING

The next healing case that demonstrates the role of Jesus as Mediator is found in Mark 10:46-52:

And they came to Jericho: and as he went out of Jericho with his disciples and a great number of people, blind Bartimaeus, the son of Timaeus sat by the highway side begging.

And when he heard that it was Jesus of Nazareth, he began to cry out, and say, Jesus, thou Son of David, have mercy on me.

And many charged him that he should hold his peace: but he cried the more a great deal, Thou Son of David, have mercy on me.

And Jesus stood still, and commanded him to be called. And they call the blind man, saying unto him, Be of good comfort, rise; he calleth thee.

And he, casting away his garment, rose, and came to Jesus.

And Jesus answered and said unto him, What wilt thou that I should do unto thee? The blind man said unto him, Lord, that I might receive my sight.

And Jesus said unto him, Go thy way; thy faith hath made thee whole. And immediately he received his sight, and followed Jesus in the way.

If we were to look to the end of this account first, we would see that faith is involved. I believe, however, that we can include this case as an example of the God-man side of healing.

Blind Bartimaeus is to be commended for understanding that Jesus was the Son of David. Calling Jesus the Son of David was to call Him the Messiah. This indicates that Bartimaeus knew whom he was addressing when he called out to Jesus for help, for most people used the human name, Jesus of Nazareth, when they talked about Him.

It is also interesting to note that the Bible doesn't record that anyone else in that gathering received a healing. We can see that Bartimaeus knew who Jesus was; however, he didn't know whether or not Jesus heard him. So Bartimaeus's cry was actually more a plea of desperation than a cry of faith.

But we do see faith in Bartimaeus, especially when he was told that Jesus heard him and he responded by throwing aside his garment. This garment was a status symbol that represented Bartimaeus's condition of blindness. The fact that Bartimaeus threw the garment away indicates he believed he wouldn't need it anymore. This is definitely faith in action. Yet when Bartimaeus came over and stood before Jesus, he was still blind.

Notice Bartimaeus's response when Jesus asked him, "What do you want Me to do for you?" Bartimaeus replied, "Teacher, that I might receive my sight." (See v. 51.)

At this point, Bartimaeus hadn't received yet. What Jesus instructed him to do next is the reason I would place this case in the God-man category. Jesus said, "Go your way; your faith has made you whole." (See v. 52.)

Notice that Jesus didn't tell Bartimaeus to follow Him; He just said, "Go your way." But how does a blind man go his way?

This is precisely why Jesus told Bartimaeus he had faith to do it. Only by faith could a blind man obey Jesus's instructions and "go his way."

Again and again Jesus encouraged people to do the very thing they couldn't do in the natural. Bartimaeus turned to obey Jesus, and his eyes immediately opened. Once healed, Bartimaeus joined the rest of the seeing crowd and joyfully followed the Master.

Bartimaeus's part was to come to Jesus and ask Him for help to obtain his healing. The part Jesus played was the role of a mediator, connecting man with God.

The Rest of the Story

As you can see, there is a definite difference between the man side and the God-man side. The man side involves faith on the part of the individual without the help of anyone else. The God-man side also involves faith, but the recipient and the minister combine to work together.

This distinction may seem very insignificant or simply a matter of semantics. But, on the contrary, it represents a great difference between these two methods of blessing.

Jesus was a master at moving people into faith and

helping them release that faith. Without His help many would have struggled to receive on their own; failing to make a connection with God.

The following list includes the fourteen other cases of healing in Jesus' ministry. I have made some brief comments about each one to help place them in their proper categories:

1. The Leper: Mark 1:40–45

God-Man Side

This man needed to know whether or not it was the will of Jesus to heal him. Without knowledge of God's will, faith has nothing to lay hold of. Or as one minister once said, "Faith begins where the will of God is known."

Jesus answered the leper's question both with His words and with the immediate touch of His healing hand.

2. Simon's Mother-in-Law: Luke 4:38–39

God-Man Side

In this situation, only the faith and anointing of Jesus were involved. No gift of the Spirit was used in rebuking a fever. This, too, was a case of the *God-man side*.

3. The Ten Lepers: Luke 17:11-19
God-Man Side

The lepers cried out for Jesus's help. Jesus gave them instructions to go and show themselves to the priests. They were healed as they obeyed.

4. The Nobleman's Son: John 4:46-54
God-Man Side

At the nobleman's request for help, Jesus commanded him to go home, assuring him that his son lived. As the man obeyed, the miracle happened.

5. The Man with the Withered Hand: Matthew 12:9-13
God-Man Side

According to Jesus's established pattern, He told the man to do something he couldn't do—to stretch out his hand. When the man did what he was told, his hand was restored.

6. The Two Blind Men: Matthew 9:27-31
Man Side or God-Man Side

The two men followed Jesus and cried out for mercy. Jesus asked them, "Do you believe I can do this?" When the men responded, "Yes," they were healed.

7. The Epileptic Boy: Mark 9:14-29
God-Man Side

The child was under the influence of a dumb and deaf spirit. Jesus cast it out. Authority was used; no gift was necessary.

8. The Blind Man at Bethsaida: Mark 8:22-26
God-Man Side

Jesus laid hands on this man twice to complete his healing. If the man's healing was simply a gift, why did Jesus lay hands on him twice? The man needed help connecting with the power of God.

9. The Woman with the "Spirit of Infirmity:" Luke 13:11-17
God-Man Side

According to verse 11, it was known that this woman had a spirit of infirmity; Jesus didn't need a gift of the Spirit to help Him discern this. He simply spoke in faith and loosed the woman so the evil spirit would leave her and her body could then become normal again. Jesus alluded to the fact that He had exercised His authority to free this woman in verse 16.

10. The Blind and Dumb Demoniac: Matthew 12:22-23
God Side or God-Man Side
Again, as in the last case, this man was known to have a devil. Luke tells us that Jesus cast the devil out. If Jesus needed a gift of the Spirit to reveal that He was dealing with a devil, this would be an example of the *God side* method of healing. If Jesus did not need such information, it would be a case of the *God-man side.*

Four more cases of healing in Jesus's ministry remain. It is difficult to draw proper conclusions about these four because the information given is not complete. In most of these cases, we leave room for error by stating that the method of healing was either God-initiated intervention or God-man mediation.

11. The Dumb Demoniac: Matthew 9:32-33
God Side or God-Man Side
Jesus cast out the devil.

12. The Blind Man at Siloam: John 9:1-38
God Side or God-Man Side
The method Jesus used to heal this man indicates that He was led by the Holy Spirit.

13. The Deaf Man with a Speech Impediment: Mark 7:31-37

God Side or God-Man Side

If Jesus took the man aside from the multitude, could this have been to allow His authority and faith to work for the man? If it were a gift, why would He need to do this? It is difficult to draw a definite conclusion.

14. The Man with Dropsy: Luke 14:1-6

God Side or God-Man Side

This case is like the one of the man with the withered hand, except that this time Jesus gave no instructions to the man.

All these cases provide us with insight into the healing ministry of the Master Mediator, Jesus Himself. If we want to measure up to the Master in ministry, we must be willing to stand in the gap for others, helping them make their connection with God so they can release their faith and see God's power manifested in their lives.

MAN SIDE/ FAITH SIDE	GOD–MAN SIDE/ MEDIATOR SIDE	GOD SIDE/ GIFT SIDE
Mark 5:25-34	Luke 5:17-25	John 5:1-9
Matthew 8:5-13	Mark 10:46-52	Matthew 9:32-33*
Matthew 9:27-31*	Mark 1:40-45	John 9:1-38*
	Luke 4:38-39	Mark 7:31-37*
	Luke 17:11-19	Luke 14:1-6*
	John 4:46-54	Matthew 12:22-23*
	Matthew 12:9-13	
	Mark 9:14-29	
	Mark 8:22-26	
	Luke 13:11-17	

*These cases could also be examples of *the God-man side.*

Chapter 4

CONSIDER WHO YOU ARE

If the body of Christ is to duplicate the ministry of Jesus, it is imperative to "rightly divide" the methods He used. As the body of Christ, we must see things as Jesus sees them, developing His perspective and adopting His mentality.

The "consciousness" of a man is what that man knows to be true. What a man knows to be true will be depicted in the man's demeanor.

Wherever Jesus went, He carried such a wonderful presence of God's Spirit. Thus, whenever Jesus came on the scene, devils cringed and cried out; religious people complained and sought to do away with Him; and, of course, the normal people who needed His help loved Him.

If we are to carry the same presence of God and duplicate the same powerful ministry of Jesus, then we must think like Him. We must understand our divine purpose and authority just as He did.

As we seek to replace our old thought patterns with Jesus's way of thinking, there is one thing we can be sure of: Jesus developed His thought life through the Word. Luke 2:40-52 NKJV gives us insight into Jesus's growth through the Word, even as a child:

> **And the Child grew and became strong in spirit, filled with wisdom; and the grace of God was upon Him.**
>
> **His parents went to Jerusalem every year at the Feast of the Passover.**
>
> **And when He was twelve years old, they went up to Jerusalem according to the custom of the feast.**
>
> **When they had finished the days, as they returned, the Boy Jesus lingered behind in Jerusalem. And Joseph and His mother did not know it;**
>
> **but supposing Him to have been in the company, they went a day's journey, and sought Him among their relatives and acquaintances.**
>
> **So when they did not find Him, they returned to Jerusalem, seeking Him.**
>
> **Now so it was that after three days they found Him in the temple, sitting in the midst of the**

teachers, both listening to them and asking them questions.

And all who heard Him were astonished at His understanding and answers.

So when they saw Him, they were amazed; and His mother said to Him, "Son, why have You done this to us? Look, Your father and I have sought You anxiously."

And He said to them, "Why did you seek Me? Did you not know that I must be about My Father's business?"

But they did not understand the statement which He spoke to them.

Then He went down with them and came to Nazareth, and was subject to them, but His mother kept all these things in her heart.

And Jesus increased in wisdom and stature, and in favor with God and men.

The main point to note in this passage is that Jesus both grew and became strong in spirit and that He increased in wisdom and stature. The words "grew," "became," and "increased" all indicate that Jesus's development was progressive.

To some, this truth comes as a real revelation. Many see Jesus only as the Son of God, fully equipped with all knowledge and revelation. However, Jesus was also human, which legally bound Him to function on the earth as a human with our complete redemption as His goal. That means if Jesus could increase in wisdom and stature and in favor with God and men, then so can we.

DEVELOPING THE MIND OF CHRIST

Philippians 2:5-6 recently caught my attention. God quickened some truths to my heart about this passage of Scripture—truths that encompass the very purpose behind this book. Verses 5 and 6 state: **Let this mind be in you, which was also in Christ Jesus: Who, being in the form of God, thought it not robbery to be equal with God.**

Of course, God would never require us to walk in something that is impossible for us to achieve. Therefore, it is entirely possible for us to have the mind of Christ.

Consider the profound importance of the mind of Christ. Solomon said, **"As he thinks in his heart, so is he"** (Proverbs 23:7 NKJV). This means without question that the body of Christ must think as Jesus thought in order to duplicate His ministry. First John 2:6 NKJV says, **He who says he abides in Him ought himself also to walk just as He walked.**

Throughout the life of Jesus, He was extremely certain of who He was. John records Jesus as saying, **"I and my**

Father are one" (John 10:30). Later in this passage of Scripture, Jesus declared, "I am the Son of God" (v. 36).

Now look at Philippians 2:6 NIV: **Who, being in very nature God, did not consider equality with God something to be grasped.**

Jesus was equal with God, but He didn't hold on to His right or the advantages of that equality. Before He entered this world to be born a man, He first laid aside all the privileges of being God. He even let go of the fact that being equal with God would in any way prevent Him from coming to fulfill His destiny.

His appearance was that of a man (v. 8); however, He would bind Himself to His humanity in order to fulfill His earthly ministry. The question we must ask is this: Since Jesus was indeed a human being in a human body with a human mind, what quality or link with the divine made possible His tremendous success and ultimate victory over death, hell, and the grave?

Immediately the answer would seem to be that Jesus was anointed with the power of the Holy Ghost. However, the body of Christ is also anointed with the power of the Holy Ghost; yet Christians consistently fail to reproduce the works of Jesus.

The apostle Paul comments on certain principles that apply to the question stated above. Philippians 2:12,13 NIV says, **Therefore, my dear friends, as you have always obeyed—not only in my presence, but now much more** in my absence—continue to work out your salvation with fear and trembling, for it is God who works in you to will and to act according to his good purpose.

Paul later states in Second Corinthians 4:7 that we have a treasure in these earthen vessels—that the excellence of the power within us is of God and not of us. Paul seems to highlight well the distinction between God and the human being within whom He dwells. Paul describes God's presence as a treasure of great value that must be manifested to the world.

As we reflect now on the life and ministry of Jesus, we must remember that before He came into the world, Jesus did not consider His equality with God something to be held on to. Yet when we review His time on the earth, we see that the majority of His considerations were focused on His heavenly estate, the anointing from heaven, His heavenly purpose, and His Father's companionship.

Jesus constantly talked about His Father. He also talked continually about who He was and what it was He was sent to accomplish. It would seem that Jesus's willingness to temporarily abandon His heavenly privileges provided access into this human world, while at the same time His continued heavenly contemplations, and corresponding action gave Him access to provision from heaven and brought the power of God upon His life into manifestation.

We see, then, that a key or link Jesus utilized to

access the power of heaven was this: *the very position He was willing to temporarily lay aside, was the truth that when in faith acted upon, would reveal the power of His purpose and the glory of His original estate.*

Consider Who You Are in Christ

Romans 6:1-11 can help us unlock this mystery:

What shall we say then? Shall we continue in sin, that grace may abound?

God forbid. How shall we, that are dead to sin, live any longer therein?

Know ye not, that so many of us as were baptized into Jesus Christ were baptized into his death?

Therefore we are buried with him by baptism into death: that like as Christ was raised up from the dead by the glory of the Father, even so we also should walk in newness of life.

For if we have been planted together in the likeness of his death, we shall be also in the likeness of his resurrection:

Knowing this, that our old man is crucified with him, that the body of sin might be destroyed, that henceforth we should not serve sin.

For he that is dead is freed from sin.

Now if we be dead with Christ, we believe that we shall also live with him:

Knowing that Christ being raised from the dead dieth no more; death hath no more dominion over him.

For in that he died, he died unto sin once: but in that he liveth, he liveth unto God.

Likewise reckon ye also yourselves to be dead indeed unto sin, but alive unto God through Jesus Christ our Lord.

As we evaluate how Paul wrote this passage in light of our original text found in Philippians 2:5, we can comprehend the significance of what Jesus was doing when He considered Himself equal or equipped for His heavenly assignment (redemption of mankind).

Paul takes the first ten verses in Romans 6 to describe what we have become in Christ and how this transformation has taken place. We call this the legal side to redemption.

Jesus has already redeemed the whole of mankind. His death, burial, and resurrection was in fact *our* death, burial, and resurrection. What He did, He did for us. When we accept this finished work, the reality of it becomes ours, and we begin to tap its benefits.

Whether or not you know it, you became free from sin the moment you were born again. Second Peter 1:3 says that all things pertaining to life and godliness are yours. Whether or not you experience those benefits in your everyday life does not make this statement any less true.

Now look at Romans 6:11. Paul tells us to reckon or consider ourselves to be dead indeed to sin and alive unto God. You might say, "But isn't that what Paul spent the last ten verses telling us?" Yes, that is correct. However, now Paul exhorts you to *experience* what it is like to be free. And the first step toward experiencing that freedom begins with what you allow yourself to consider.

Look at that key word "consider." In order to work out your salvation, you must *consider* yourself to be who God says you are. After all, why would you take the time to consider anything in the first place? You do so because what you consider may be different than what appears to be true.

God told Joshua to meditate day and night on the Word of God in order to become effective in performing the will of God (Joshua 1:8). But, what about Jesus? Do you think He took the time to consider who He was? Absolutely. Remember, Jesus acted as a man while on the earth. He lived in a human body with a human mind; therefore, it was necessary for Him to consider who He really was in order for Him to function according to the fullest capacity available to Him as a man anointed by the Spirit of God.

John 10:30-32 NKJV shows us that Jesus was established in who He was because He considered or acknowledged who He was according to God's purpose for Him.

"I and My Father are one."

Then the Jews took up stones again to stone Him.

Jesus answered them, "Many good works I have shown you from My Father. For which of those works do you stone Me?"

Notice again that Jesus validates who He is by the works being done.

As I thought about this one day, the thought occurred to me that it would be interesting to turn this passage around. Yes, Jesus set forth His works to authenticate who He was. But was it also possible that He was able to produce those works only because He had first considered Himself to be equal with God?

This makes perfect sense. Jesus is God, yet if He wanted to express and demonstrate that truth on this earth, He first had to consider it to be so. Jesus was revealing the divine treasure of who He was through His earthly being.

Thus, the demonstrations of God's power that we might assume to be an inevitable part of Jesus's ministry were in fact a by-product of His considerations. Jesus was filled with power, yet the power worked because Jesus *knew* it would. Remember, Proverbs 23:7 NKJV says, **For as he** [a man] **thinks in his heart, so is he.**

How easy it is to conclude that Jesus did all that He

did on this earth because He is Jesus. However, if He had to use His mind to facilitate the anointing so He could act in faith, then we must do the same.

MAN'S CALL TO EXERCISE DOMINION

When we consider the works of Jesus, we can see a progression in the actual working out of what He knew. First Corinthians 15:45 states that Jesus was the last Adam. It would seem that one of the primary purposes of the last Adam was to fulfill and correct the work of the *first* Adam. Romans 5:18 NKJV makes mention that, **therefore, as through one man's offense judgment came to all men, resulting in condemnation, even so through one Man's righteous act the free gift came to all men, resulting in justification of life.**

Part of the first Adam's responsibility was to exercise dominion over the earth that God had made for man:

And God said, Let us make man in our image, after our likeness: and let them have dominion over the fish of the sea, and over the fowl of the air, and over the cattle, and over all the earth, and over every creeping thing that creepeth upon the earth.

Genesis 1:26

Immediately after God created man, He gave him dominion. Adam was to rule over everything God had created, which included everything that breathed upon the earth. Adam was the first king of the beasts, and more. However, all this authority was lost when man submitted himself to Satan.

As we watch Jesus in His earth walk, we see Him exercise dominion as if it were a lost skill:

And he was there in the wilderness forty days, tempted of Satan; and was with the wild beasts; and the angels ministered unto him.

Mark 1:13

The first area of influence that Jesus created was over the wild beasts. (Interestingly, Mark was the only Gospel writer to mention this incident; the others failed to do so.) Notice that it doesn't say Jesus was out in the field with a puppy dog and a pussycat. He was in the desert with hungry, wild beasts. The obvious reason He didn't become their lunch is that He had dominion and authority over them.

The next opportunity for Jesus to reveal who He was came in the same desert when He defeated the temptations of the devil. God designed man never to lose a battle. Jesus showed us how it is possible, for He was the "Word become flesh":

And the Word became flesh and dwelt among us, and we beheld His glory, the glory as of the only begotten of the Father, full of grace and truth.

John 1:14 NKJV

As you read the Gospels, notice an amazing progression of developed awareness in Jesus. In the booklet entitled, "The Truth about Divine Healing," John G. Lake wrote:

In beginning His revelation of the life of God for and in man, Jesus chose the order of nature as the realm of His first demonstration (1) Jesus turned the water into wine, (2) He stilled the waves, (3) He walked on water. These revelations of power over nature each surpassed the other.

Then Jesus astounded His followers by turning to the creative life of God. He fed the multitude by an act of creative power when He created fish and bread to feed five thousand.

This shows the distinction between healings and miracles. Miracles are creative. Healing is a restoration of what has been.

Jesus now advances into a new sphere, the order of sickness. Here He meets the mind of the other that must be conformed to His. (1) Jesus heals Peter's mother-in-law. This is first degree healing.

(2) Jesus meets the blind man and heals him. This is second degree healing. (3) The lepers are healed. Healing in the third degree.

Again Jesus enters the creative realm and creates eyes in a man born blind. Blindness from birth is evidence of an unfinished condition of the eyes. The creative process was not complete. Jesus stooped, took dust from the road, spat upon it and put it on the man's eyes. In so doing, He finished a work of creation—the man saw.

Jesus again advances. This time He chooses the order of death. (1) He raised the daughter of Jairus, dead a few minutes. This is the first degree. (2) Jesus meets a funeral procession coming out of the city of Nain. He commands the young man to live, "and he sat up." This man was dead many hours. This is the second degree. (3) He commanded His friend Lazarus to come forth. He that was dead four days arose. This was the third degree.

Now Jesus again steps into the creative realm and announces His coming death. He declares of life: "I have the power to lay it down, and I have power to take it again."

Through this chain of successive abandonment to God we discover the soul-steps of Jesus. Every step was taken with reliance upon the Word of God as the all-sufficient guide. "Is it possbile that Jesus wanted to raise up Lazarus being dead 4 days so His soul could experience mastery over death and thereby conceptualize the raising of Himself in 3 days?[2]"

The next few chapters will examine how we as believers can adopt this understanding. In this examination, the Gospel of John will be the focus of our attention.

For some time now, the Lord has had me interested in the gospel of John. Everywhere Jesus spoke, I find myself analyzing His words in light of what He knew at the time He spoke. Why did Jesus say the things He said, and what did He know that made Him so sure?

As I have studied the epistles, I have come to realize more and more how important it is that we discover the answers to these questions. One of the most emphasized words in the Pauline epistles is the word "know." Paul was extremely interested in the church's having knowledge. He risked his life to be in dangerous company just to reaffirm the faith of certain believers. Paul even sent associate ministers to different groups of people to check up on their beliefs.

Perhaps the apostle Paul was so interested in continually providing important information because he knew that without constantly reminding believers of their role as Christians, they would cease to produce results.

How important, then, is our goal of learning to think like Jesus? Would it be conceivable to duplicate the ministry of Jesus if it were possible to understand what He knew?

Chapter 5

BEHOLD THE GLORY
OF GOD IN YOU

Let this mind be in you which was also in
Christ Jesus.

Philippians 2:5 NKJV

O ur journey through Jesus's thought processes will
not only reveal and unveil secrets in the realm of
God, but it will also provoke examination of our
own religious temperaments.

Religion and tradition have a way of hiding and
avoiding the discovery of truth. However, Paul said that
even though the god of this world blinds the minds of
men, the glorious light of the gospel shining upon them
will reveal truth (2 Corinthians 4:4).

The Light of Eternal Life

John 1:1-5 NKJV says this light that dispels darkness and reveals truth finds its origin in Jesus:

> **In the beginning was the Word, and the Word was with God, and the Word was God.**
>
> **He was in the beginning with God.**
>
> **All things were made through Him, and without Him nothing was made that was made.**
>
> **In Him was life, and the life was the light of men.**
>
> **And the light shines in the darkness, and the darkness did not comprehend it.**

To think like God is to adopt a biblical belief until that belief actually represents the person who has adopted it.

According to verse 1 of this passage in John, the Word *exists with* God, and the Word also *accompanies* God. Most importantly, however, the Word *is* God.

You may have a Bible and carry it with you, but do you believe the Word to be *a part of* you? Are you one with the Word? If you are not convinced of the Word, that Word will not be established in you or demonstrated through your life.

Already we are being challenged to think of our relationship with the Lord in the context of two becoming one. We will no longer be able to consider our standing in

Christ as somehow distinct from Him. From this point on, we must accept our union with Christ as inseparable.

Jesus's life—eternal life—was poured into *our* lives, and the light of eternal life now radiates and lives in us. This life and light then becomes our spiritual immune system for the rest of our time on this earth. As Paul said, **Old things have passed away; behold, all things have become new** (2 Corinthians 5:17 NKJV). Even the darkness of Satan's activity, so persistent in its pursuit of control over our lives, cannot overcome this newfound eternal life that is in us now that we belong to Christ.

YIELDING TO YOUR NEW NATURE

The majority of all that will be said in the next few chapters are statements intended for meditation. You can make them more real to you by saying these statements of faith out loud, praising the Lord about them, and speaking in other tongues while meditating on them throughout the day.

For example, consider John 1:12-14 NKJV, which continues to speak about Jesus as the Word of God:

> **But as many as received Him, to them He gave the right to become children of God, to those who believe in His name:**

Who were born, not of blood, nor of the will of the flesh, nor of the will of man, but of God.

And the Word became flesh and dwelt among us, and we beheld His glory, the glory as of the only begotten of the Father, full of grace and truth.

When an individual receives Jesus, God gives that person power to become something. As John G. Lake said, "Being always precedes doing." God has given you power to become something you were not before; therefore, you can do something you could not do before. In fact, Paul said you can do *all* things through Christ who strengthens you! (Philippians 4:13).

Can you see the great need for the born-again man to yield to his new nature?

In John 1:13, we see that we are no longer to be associated with the nature of the man born of human blood according to the will of the flesh or the will of man. In fact, it almost seems as if one of the worst things we can do after being born again is to think of ourselves as mere natural humans. We are to consider ourselves to be born of God.

Of course, we *are* human but now only in part. First and foremost, we must consider the recreation of our human spirits. We are no longer sin-nature beings. We have become recipients of God's divine nature with all the potential that entails. And as if that were not enough, God has chosen to make His home in us through the Person of

the Holy Spirit, loving us and assisting us in the fulfillment of His orchestrated plan for this world.

Will the real sons of God please step forward? This is the
unconscious heart cry of a lost world, for people have yet
to see a church that fully represents Jesus the way He
walked on this earth. *But they will.* The spiritual giant
called the church is now awakening to occupy its rightful
place and to walk out its divine purpose in these last days
before Jesus returns.

In chapter 1, verse 14, John goes on to reveal the
destiny of the church. Just as the Word became flesh and
dwelt among us, so again the Word has been made flesh
in the form of the church. The body of Christ is the
flesh-and-blood temple God has chosen to inhabit on the
earth in order to bring about His plan and purpose for
the world. Therefore, we can emphatically say, "God *still*
dwells among us!" Or as Paul says in Galatians 2:20 (the
Distilled translation), **I have died, and I am now enjoying
my second existence, which is simply Jesus using my
body.**[3]

BEHOLDING HIS GLORY IN OUR LIVES

John goes on to say, **(and we beheld his glory, the glory as
of the only begotten of the Father,) full of grace and
truth** (John 1:14). This is where the church needs to step

out of all its religious and traditional boxes. After all, God was never in those boxes anyway!

Thank God for all the glory that is to be revealed in these last days. However, why wait? When the Word becomes flesh and dwells with us, the potential for beholding God's glory is available to us *now*.

Remember: When God moves in, you become a move. When you move, God does too.

Notice what else John says in this verse—that *we* are filled with grace and truth. Grace is God's ability to do for us what we cannot do ourselves.

Truth is by definition reality; therefore, the package is complete. God inhabits our fleshly being. As a result, the glory of God is beheld in human form. This is possible because of God's ability or grace and heaven's definition of reality. We can see that we are to manifest Christ on the earth. If we will *think* this way, we can *act* this way.

WE ARE TO INTRODUCE JESUS TO THE WORLD

As we continue to view ourselves in light of the life and ministry of Jesus, John gives us another piece to the puzzle in John 1:18:

> **No man hath seen God at any time; the only begotten Son, which is in the bosom of the Father, he hath declared him.**

One meaning of the word "declared" is *to make clear.*[4] Jesus had the job of making the Father clear to the world. This means we, too, have the responsibility of making Jesus clear to the world.

In John 14:7-12 NKJV, Jesus had a discussion with His disciples concerning this issue:

> "If you had known Me, you would have known My Father also; and from now on you know Him and have seen Him."
>
> Philip said to Him, "Lord, show us the Father, and it is sufficient for us."
>
> Jesus said to him, "Have I been with you so long, and yet you have not known Me, Philip? He who has seen Me has seen the Father; so how can you say, 'Show us the Father'?
>
> "Do you not believe that I am in the Father, and the Father in Me? The words that I speak to you I do not speak on My own authority; but the Father who dwells in Me does the works.
>
> "Believe Me that I am in the Father and the Father in Me, or else believe Me for the sake of the works themselves.
>
> "Most assuredly, I say to you, he who believes in Me, the works that I do he will do also; and greater works than these he will do, because I go to My Father."

There is a specific reason Jesus said in verse 12 that we who believe in Him will do the same works He did. He wanted to direct our attention to the necessity of following after the pattern He established in the previous verses. In the same way Jesus used His works to bring validity to His message, we, too, must produce results to convince the world that Jesus lives.

Are we willing to say, "If you have seen me, you have seen Jesus"? This is the extent to which we must be willing to have others compare us against the truth of God's Word, which calls us to be conformed to the image of Christ in all things.

Paul's revelation to the church continually challenged the hearers to be conformed to the image of Christ. We will never be conformed through "mind over matter," so something else must be present in a tangible way to produce the desired result. Thank God, the living Christ Himself is present, having taken up residence within our hearts through the Person of the Holy Spirit.

Now we are to be one with Him—flesh of His flesh and bone of His bones. Just as Eve was made from the same natural substance as Adam, so we have been made from the same spiritual substance as Jesus. Once we understand this truth and consider it to be so, the eternal life *within* us will begin to manifest *through* us.

How could it get any better than this? God's provision for us is so rich and plentiful, it is beyond our ability to comprehend. Because of that divine provision, we have the privilege of allowing God to find expression through us on this earth. And as we utilize what God has provided for us to do the works of Jesus—teaching, preaching, and healing—we meet His standard by which the world is to know that Jesus is alive.

JESUS'S SUPREME CONFIDENCE IN THE SUPERNATURAL

There are a few additional thoughts I want to add. It is found in John 1:50-51 NKJV and concerns Jesus's response to Nathanael, who proclaimed Him to be the king of Israel simply because Jesus said He had seen Nathanael under a fig tree before they met.

> **Jesus answered and said to him, "Because I said to you, 'I saw you under the fig tree,' do you believe? You will see greater things than these."**
> **And He said to him, "Most assuredly, I say to you, hereafter you shall see heaven open, and the angels of God ascending and descending upon the Son of Man."**

Notice how real the supernatural realm was to Jesus. He knew of the greater things in God. He was confident that what had been witnessed was only a prelude to the miraculous. He even stated that heaven would open on His behalf and that there would be angelic assistance for what He had to accomplish.

As we continue our study of the book of John, we will find that Jesus's bold statements only increase. But here in this first chapter, it's already obvious that Jesus displayed tremendous confidence in the supernatural. This is the same state of mind and place in God every Christian is ordained to occupy.

Can you see that angels are ordained by God to assist your life? Is it beginning to dawn on your heart that the heavens are opened unto you and that greater demonstrations of God's power than this world has seen thus far are available for you to operate in? Will you begin to comprehend and act on these truths? And when God begins to move mightily in your life, will you be stunned with disbelief, or will you be pleased with the fruit of your expectations?

As we begin to study the second chapter of John's gospel, you may still be contemplating the challenging questions in the previous paragraph. If need be, stop and meditate on these thoughts while the Holy Ghost has your attention.

You see, the Spirit of God can do marvelous things when He has the attention of your spirit and soul at the same time. Whenever you contemplate or meditate on a truth in God's Word and a certain truth leaps out at you, stop and muse over it.

The mind is so fickle; if you allow it to dart back and forth, it will never focus or be still. So capture your mind's attention and harness the truth that arouses your curiosity. Then allow your imagination to role-play the impossible.

ACCESSING THE MIRACULOUS

The second chapter of John mentions the historic beginning of miracles in Jesus's ministry. Jesus attended a wedding in Cana where His mother, Mary, had apparently been actively involved.

> **And when they ran out of wine, the mother of Jesus said to Him, "They have no wine."**
>
> **Jesus said to her, "Woman, what does your concern have to do with Me? My hour has not yet come."**
>
> **His mother said to the servants, "Whatever He says to you, do it."**
>
> **John 2:3-5 NKJV**

When the wine ran out at the wedding in Cana to which Jesus and His mother had been invited, immediately Mary responded with great concern.

One day I was pondering why Mary was so busy in the matters of this wedding. As I endeavored to put myself in her place and then imagine the intricate possibilities of the entire scenario, I began to see something.

First of all, if I were a guest at a wedding enjoying the feast, I would not necessarily be very knowledgeable about the problems faced by the kitchen staff. I might eventually notice an inconvenience; however, if I hadn't been given the proper authority, I would be unable to do anything about it.

Notice the concern Mary displayed. Only a member of the staff or someone in charge would be as concerned as she was. I therefore believe Mary must have been the wedding coordinator. She was responsible for everything that was happening, and her goal was to help produce a glorious wedding.

As the coordinator, Mary knew the current status of the wine cellar. So when the wine ran out, she looked for a solution beyond the natural to the supernatural. In other words, she turned to her Son Jesus and brought the situation to His attention.

Jesus recognized who had authority and who didn't. That is why He replied, **"Woman, what does your concern have to do with Me?"** (v. 4). As long as Mary clung to her authority in the matter, Jesus was limited.

But notice what Mary then said to the servants: **Whatever He says to you, do it** (v. 5). Who has the right to order someone else's servants around? It is obvious to me that Mary had a position of authority in this situation.

Once the baton was passed, Jesus could go to work. I find it interesting that Jesus didn't drop to His knees and begin to pray, nor did He teach for an hour so the anointing could be present. Jesus simply gave a command to the servants:

> Now there were set six waterpots of stone, according to the manner of purification of the Jews, containing twenty or thirty gallons apiece.
>
> Jesus said to them, "Fill the waterpots with water." And they filled them up to the brim.
>
> And He said to them, "Draw some out now, and take it to the master of the feast." And they took it.
>
> When the master of the feast had tasted the water that was made wine, and did not know where it came from (but the servants who had drawn the water knew), the master of the feast called the bridegroom.
>
> And he said to him, "Every man at the beginning sets out the good wine, and when the guests have well drunk, then the inferior. You have kept the good wine until now!"
>
> This beginning of signs Jesus did in Cana of Galilee, and manifested His glory; and His disciples believed in Him.
>
> **John 2:6-11** NKJV

Jesus knew that *the anointing is accessed by obedience to directions.*

SEE PROBLEMS AS NEW OPPORTUNITIES FOR YOUR FAITH

Here's a very important point to note: *the problem was never really a problem.* This is often true in many situations of life. This is what Smith Wigglesworth meant when he said, "You can never pray the prayer of faith while looking at the problem."

To Jesus, the required miracle was not the difficulty. His efforts were focused on connecting the obedience of people with His cooperation with the Holy Spirit. Once the directions were obeyed and His instructions were implemented, the miracle began.

Let me ask you a few questions here that will help you locate yourself in this matter of turning an obstacle into a miracle:

- How confident are you in God?
- What do you believe about the unseen realm?
- How big is the problem to you?
- If you sensed the Holy Spirit leading you to tell someone to do something that he or she could not do in the natural, would you obey?

To the individual who is focused on his or her problems, there are always problems. The way that person perceives his situation determines the outcome of those difficulties.

Remember back in grade school when the teacher would ask for volunteers to work the problems on the chalkboard? The "problem" was a real problem only when someone didn't have the answer to it.

Can you see the importance of perspective? If you see your problems as opportunities that are easily solved by the abundance of God's ability, you have a healthy perspective. The attitude with which you approach your difficulties will always determine the success of your outcome.

Jesus simply said to the servants, "Fill up the waterpots." I believe the ready obedience of the servants had to do with the confident demeanor of Jesus, for confidence is contagious. Notice what a good job the servants did. They filled those pots up right to the brim!

Next, Jesus said, "Draw some out and give it to the master of the feast." If Jesus had failed to produce a miracle, His failure could have cost those servants their jobs or even their lives. But the confident authority of Jesus, whom they did not know, inspired something within the servants that was greater than the fear of failing their master, whom they did know.

An onlooker might say, "What a risk those servants took!" Herein lies the secret to the miraculous realm: *the ability to transmit faith from one person to another.*

Jesus was a master at transmitting faith to others. He carried such a sense of authority and exuded such confidence in every situation that people were lifted into one accord with His faith just by being in His presence.

As the servants obeyed Jesus's instructions, somewhere between the waterpot and the master's cup the water turned into wine.

What a privilege it is to sit at the Master's feet and learn the art of conversion! In the natural realm, we learn about conversion when we go into another country and have to convert our money into the currency of that country. But that same principle, when applied to the spiritual realm, can transform every difficulty into a testimony of overcoming victory. As we learn from the ministry of Jesus, we will come to understand how to convert our faith into heaven's currency of miracles, signs, and wonders.

GOD'S ZEALOUS CARE FOR HIS LIVING TEMPLES

Before leaving John chapter 2, we need to look at the way Jesus viewed the temple of God:

> Now the Passover of the Jews was at hand, and Jesus went up to Jerusalem.
> And He found in the temple those who sold

oxen and sheep and doves, and the money changers doing business.

When He had made a whip of cords, He drove them all out of the temple, with the sheep and the oxen, and poured out the changers' money and overturned the tables.

And He said to those who sold doves, "Take these things away! Do not make My Father's house a house of merchandise!"

Then His disciples remembered that it was written, "Zeal for Your house has eaten Me up."

John 2:13-17 NKJV

You as the reader must continue to understand that the thoughts, the words, and the actions of our Lord are for our admonition. Considering what Jesus considered, thinking as Jesus thought, and acting as Jesus acted will produce exactly the same results that Jesus Himself produced.

The course of action Jesus took is understood by the statement, **Zeal for your house has eaten me up**, or as the *New International Version* says, **Zeal for your house will consume me** (v. 17). The word "consumed" is translated from the Greek *katesthio* or *kataphago*, meaning "to devour, that is, to squander, to waste: substance, to strip one of his goods, to ruin (by the infliction of injuries), used of the consumption of the strength of body and mind by strong emotions."[5]

It is quite obvious that God is serious about His place of residence. "Zeal" here means "zealous excitement of mind, ardor, fervor of spirit."[6] In this passage, the emphasis is on an envious and contentious rivalry or jealousy.

James 4:5 NKJV also speaks of God in this manner: **Or do you think that the Scripture says in vain, "The Spirit who dwells in us yearns jealously"?** The meaning of the word "jealously" here is also strong; it means "the desire to deprive another of what he has."[7] God will not put up with anyone or anything moving in on His possessions without His permission.

Jesus was and is the divine expression of His Father. Therefore, we can see the zeal of God for His house portrayed in this passage. Today *we* are His house, the temple of the living God. God is consumed with the well-being of those He has recreated in the image of His Son. That is why Paul's words were so strong in 1 Corinthians 3:16-17 NKJV:

> **Do you not know that you are the temple of God and that the Spirit of God dwells in you?**
>
> **If anyone defiles the temple of God, God will destroy him. For the temple of God is holy, which temple you are.**

Isn't it comforting to view God's justice toward His temple as we watch Jesus driving out all wickedness from its holy courts? Those who were selling and buying in the temple represent the works of the devil that continually try to defile our lives. First John 3:8 NKJV tells us that just as Jesus drove out the moneychangers from His holy temple, He zealously drives out the works of the enemy as we submit to Him:

> **He who sins is of the devil, for the devil has sinned from the beginning. For this purpose the Son of God was manifested, that He might destroy the works of the devil.**

Jesus did drive out the devil from our lives. Through His death, burial, and resurrection, He spoiled principalities and paralyzed the devil. He put the enemy under our feet so that we, the church, could live triumphantly (Colossians 2:15).

As we relate these thoughts to the finished work of redemption, we see how much God desires to bless us continually. So much can be said about the redemptive work Jesus completed for our sakes. However, redemption must still be enforced—hence, the title of this book, *Until I Come*.

Jesus desires for us to take our place as His church against every opposition. We have already legally won this fight through Christ. We need only to enforce His victory.

Are you sensing the same desire that Jesus experienced to "cleanse the temple"? Of course, this means you must first cleanse your own temple. Only then will you be able to drive out wickedness when it seeks to defile and help with the cleansing of other temples.

A mighty work must be done, but thank God, the battle has already been won!

Chapter 6

HEAVENLY THOUGHTS

John chapter 3 is a wonderful portion of Scripture that reveals mysteries differentiating heavenly things from earthly things. It constantly reminds us that no conscious thought of Jesus is ever to be taken for granted. His thoughts must become the established mentality of the church.

> There was a man of the Pharisees named Nicodemus, a ruler of the Jews.
> This man came to Jesus by night and said to Him, "Rabbi, we know that You are a teacher come from God; for no one can do these signs that You do unless God is with him."
> Jesus answered and said to him, "Most assuredly, I say to you, unless one is born again, he cannot see the kingdom of God."

Nicodemus said to Him, "How can a man be born when he is old? Can he enter a second time into his mother's womb and be born?"

Jesus answered, "Most assuredly, I say to you, unless one is born of water and the Spirit, he cannot enter the kingdom of God.

"That which is born of the flesh is flesh, and that which is born of the Spirit is spirit.

"Do not marvel that I said to you, 'You must be born again.'

"The wind blows where it wishes, and you hear the sound of it, but cannot tell where it comes from and where it goes. So is everyone who is born of the Spirit."

John 3:1-8 NKJV

At the beginning of this chapter, we see Jesus engaged in conversation with a religious leader of the synagogue named Nicodemus. The way Jesus begins His conversation indicates that He may have been looking forward to a time of fellowship with this man. Nicodemus was a student of Scripture, so it is very likely that Jesus considered his grasp of theology to be greater than most.

To See as Jesus Sees

Jesus began by telling Nicodemus, "You must be born again." Sense-ruled men cannot comprehend spiritual realities.

However, instead of comprehending the scope of Jesus's statement, Nicodemus reverted to familiar ground through rationalization. He reasoned, *Of course a man cannot be born again; that's preposterous!*

Thus, Jesus caused Nicodemus to first identify his own level of spiritual understanding. Then Jesus, the master teacher, began to make a series of simple statements in an attempt to help Nicodemus comprehend the spiritual significance of the new birth.

The church today is still like Nicodemus in some ways. Although we have accepted the need to be born again, we have stopped short of embracing the fullness of all that is available to us through that miraculous experience.

Oh, to see as Jesus sees!

In Paul's letter to the Corinthians, he wrote, **"Eye has not seen, nor ear heard, nor have entered into the heart of man the things which God has prepared for those who love Him"** (1 Corinthians 2:9 NKJV). Paul wrote a similar thought in Ephesians 3:20-21 NKJV:

Now to Him who is able to do exceedingly

abundantly above all that we ask or think, according to the power that works in us,

To Him be glory in the church by Christ Jesus to all generations for ever and ever. Amen.

The big picture is awesome. To comprehend it is to know the Holy Spirit. Thank God for His help!

In John 3:10 NKJV, Jesus raised the question to Nicodemus, "**Are you the teacher of Israel, and do not know these things?**" With Israel's rich heritage we would think that one who studied the Scriptures daily might at least recognize truth when he saw it. Jesus also talked with other religious leaders the same way in John 5:39 NKJV: "**You search the Scriptures, for in them you think you have eternal life; and these are they which testify of Me.**"

Of course, there is no way to draw a perfect parallel between the religious leaders of Jesus's day and members of the body of Christ today since those religious leaders were under the Old Covenant. However, it still would benefit us to ask these questions:

- Is it possible that even when we study and search the New Testament, we continue to miss a great deal?
- When we talk, do we speak from what we know to be true in light of the whole counsel of God,

or do we speak in light of what our denominational traditions promote?

- Could it be that we are not yet grasping certain spiritual truths that are right before us? Like Nicodemus, are we failing to comprehend the significance of these truths?

SPEAK WHAT YOU KNOW

Jesus delved deeper into spiritual truths John 3:11-12 NKJV when He said the following to Nicodemus:

> **"Most assuredly, I say to you, We speak what We know and testify what We have seen, and you do not receive Our witness.**
> **"If I have told you earthly things and you do not believe, how will you believe if I tell you heavenly things?"**

Jesus established a precedent for ministry here as He informed Nicodemus that *when He spoke, He spoke what He knew and testified about what He had seen.*

It is so important how we speak to others, for there is a huge difference between the *information* of the Word and the *inspiration* of the Word. We need both in order to be effective for God.

We must know what to believe and what not to believe, how we should think and how we should not think, and what we can do and what we cannot do. However, all of this should be soaked in inspiration. The spirit behind the information is what motivates us to do something with what we have heard.

Recently as I was talking with a friend concerning her ministry to a sick person, the Lord revealed a nugget of His truth to my heart. Among other things, I mentioned that when she ministered the Word to this person, she should do it in a particular way. Out of my heart came these words: "When you read her the Word, don't let her believe according to tradition. Cause her to believe what you know the Bible is actually saying rather than allowing her to believe it according to her religious mind-set."

Many times people fail to receive what they need from God because they hear and believe His words through the distorted filter of religion and the traditions of men.

When we know truth or can testify to its validity, we carry the persuasive ability to make others believe us.

And they were astonished at his doctrine: for he taught them as one that had authority, and not as the scribes.

Mark 1:22

Notice that both Jesus and the scribes taught. The difference was in *the way* Jesus taught. He was one with the words He spoke; they were real to Him. The outcome of His words was absolutely certain. On the contrary, the scribes taught, but not with the evidence to back up what they were saying. Their words were empty.

A well-known minister was asked the question, "Why is it that those who preach what you preach are not getting the results you are getting?" This was his response: "Because I am a voice, and they are an echo."

A Voice or an Echo?

Do you see the importance of what is being said? When you truly know something or have testified to something out of your own experience, you are a voice. What you say will carry the weight of success. On the other hand, if you are afraid to speak with conviction—if you will not dare to declare what can be expected—you are exhibiting the characteristics of an echo.

With great conviction, some will bring people right to the door of God's demonstrated power, yet they will fail to convert the listener; these are the people who are merely echoes.

Boldness is the sign of a voice, and timidity is the sign of an echo. That is why Paul, one of the greatest voices in the history of the church, endeavored to move Timothy into results by exhorting him, "God has not given you a spirit of fear [or we could also say, a spirit of timidity]." (2 Timothy 1:7.)

Simply put, an echo will have a form of religion but will deny the power. Everything he preaches might sound so good, yet no proof will follow to validate his words.

The truths Jesus gave to Nicodemus in these verses were simple but crucial to understand if we are to do the works of Jesus in this earth. Once I realized this, I immediately began to confess to myself, "I always speak what I know and testify to what I see. I am ever knowing and seeing the ways of God."

Beloved, getting these truths to work for ourselves or for others is a matter of knowing and believing them with conviction. The writings of Jesus are filled with this mentality. To work the works of Jesus, we must think as He thought.

BECOME "HEAVENLY MINDED"

In John 3:12, Jesus made a great distinction between heavenly and earthly things. In light of this, it is interesting to note what the apostle Paul said in Colossians 3:2 NKJV: **Set your minds on things above, not on things on the earth.**

This goes along with what Paul said in Second Corinthians 4:18:

While we look not at the things which are seen, but at the things which are not seen: for the things which are seen are temporal; but the things which are not seen are eternal.

Heaven became our home when we were born again. That means we are no longer strangers and foreigners, but fellow citizens with the saints and members of the household of God. (See Ephesians. 2:19.) As citizens of heaven, we need to become familiar with "the law of the land."

Heavenly things are far more weighty and real to the heavenly-minded individual. As he exposes sense-ruled knowledge to the light of truth, he recognizes that knowledge to be meager, earthly, second rate, and insubstantial. The more he considers heavenly realities rather than natural circumstances, the more his confidence becomes apparent to all.

Studying the Master will place us in direct contact with the realm of heaven. Jesus explained why in John 3:13 NKJV: **"No one has ascended to heaven but He who came down from heaven, that is, the Son of Man who is in heaven."**

Have you ever played with a yo-yo? The continual up and down motion could make you dizzy. So it seems to be with this verse. Jesus ascended to heaven and then came down, and while here He says He is there.

But making sense of this verse is easier than you might think. While Jesus walked on this earth, He lived out of heaven. In other words, Jesus lived with a continual awareness of heaven and of the eternal life within Him.

If you begin to consider the life and ministry of Jesus in light of this revelation, you can see that indeed Jesus stayed conscious of heaven at all times. This then is the secret to His steady success.

Have you ever heard the saying, "They are so heavenly minded that they are no earthly good"? In truth, unless we *are* heavenly minded, we will be no earthly good.

FULLY SUBMITTED TO THE FATHER'S WILL

The life of Jesus is fascinating to study. He had tremendous focus. He was always about His Father's business, always intent on fulfilling the will of God. He wasn't so serious that He didn't enjoy life, yet He wasn't so frivolous that He lost His sense of direction and purpose.

Joy is a notable trait that Jesus displayed in His relationship with the Father. He enjoyed His fellowship with God, and His conversations with others were often marked with accolades of His Father.

It is also very evident that Jesus paid close attention to what was going on in heaven:

Then Jesus answered and said to them, "Most assuredly, I say to you, the Son can do nothing of Himself, but what He sees the Father do; for whatever He does, the Son also does in like manner.

"For the Father loves the Son, and shows Him all things that He Himself does; and He will show Him greater works than these, that you may marvel."

John 5:19-20 NKJV

This speaks of the tremendous commitment Jesus had made to the Father. The Son of God was in total submission to the authority of His Father. Jesus realized that His success was completely in the Father's hands. Therefore, He refused to do anything other than what He observed the Father do.

This is a great truth for us to understand. Remember, as we understand how Jesus thought and then implement those thoughts into our lives, we will begin to experience the same results He did in *our* lives. Therefore, we must remain dependent on the Father at all times, just as Jesus did.

Three key qualities marked Jesus's ministry on this earth:

1. His reliance on His Father's ability rather than on His own
2. His vast comprehension of spiritual realities
3. His determination to remain focused on His

assignment without neglecting His love for the people

These three qualities—dependence on God's ability, comprehension of spiritual realities, and love for the people—must mark our expression of Jesus's ministry on this earth as well.

In John 6:38, Jesus said, **I came down from heaven, not to do mine own will, but the will of him that sent me.** Even John the Baptist picked up on the trail of His success, as we see in his words as recorded in John 3:30-36 TLB:

> "He must become greater and greater, and I must become less and less.
>
> "He has come from heaven and is greater than anyone else. I am of the earth, and my understanding is limited to the things of earth.
>
> He tells what he has seen and heard, but how few believe what he tells them!
>
> Those who believe him discover that God is a fountain of truth. For this one—sent by God—speaks God's words, for God's Spirit is upon him without measure or limit.
>
> The Father loves this man because he is his Son, and God has given him everything there is.
>
> And all who trust him—God's Son—to save them have eternal life; those who don't believe

and obey him shall never see heaven, but the wrath of God remains upon them."

John recognized that Jesus was different from any other man. Jesus had come from heaven and was therefore superior to those on the earth. Jesus was quoted often as saying that He was aware of His true origin. He knew that He had come from the Father in heaven and that He was soon to return.

John also says that Jesus told what He had seen and heard. The *Message* translation of the Bible expounds even further on this thought:

"He sets out the evidence of what he saw and heard in heaven. No one wants to deal with these facts. But anyone who examines this evidence will come to stake his life on this: that God himself is the truth."

John 3:32-33

Never was Jesus's submission to the will of the Father more evident than in the Garden of Gethsemane, where Jesus represented man's struggle with the will of the flesh and the will of God. Three times He prayed that the bitter cup would pass from Him.

That cup symbolized what Jesus would have to endure in order to purchase our redemption. In order to take His place as the substitute for mankind, Jesus had to become sin and to suffer its penalty: separation from the Father.

But each time Jesus prayed, He submitted His will to the Father's will. He kept doing this until He had overcome the desires of His own soul and flesh and fully submitted Himself in obedience to the Father. Only then was He able to complete the plan of redemption despite the suffering He was about to endure.

The outcome we see in the ministry of Jesus is what the church longs for and what the world must see in order to turn and serve Him. This is why the church must also decide to submit to the will of God, no matter what the cost. We must always choose to see and hear the will of God and submit to it through His Word and by His Spirit.

Proclaim Your Covenant Rights

I continually meditate on and confess the truth that I always see and hear the will of heaven. Oh, that we the church would wake up to see the significance of our covenant rights and privileges through Jesus Christ!

When we truly comprehend who we are in Christ and submit ourselves entirely to the authority of His Word, faith will be inspired in those who hear and see us. Then, like Jesus, we will experience the power of God flowing through our lives in a measure beyond anything we have ever known!

Chapter 7

THE SPIRIT WITHOUT MEASURE

For since He Whom God has sent speaks the words of God [proclaims God's own message], God does not give Him His Spirit sparingly or by measure, but boundless is the gift God makes of His Spirit!

John 3:34 AMP

This passage presents two vital elements that must be present in order to do the works of Jesus—the *Word of God* and the *Spirit of God.* We must understand how to cooperate with both if we are going to take our place in fulfilling God's purposes on the earth.

Throughout the Gospels, the writers emphasize that when Jesus spoke, He spoke the words of God. Peter states in 1 Peter 4:11 NKJV that we are called to do the same:

> If anyone speaks, let him speak as the oracles
> of God. If anyone ministers, let him do it as with
> the ability which God supplies, that in all things
> God may be glorified through Jesus Christ, to
> whom belong the glory and the dominion forever
> and ever. Amen.

When a person speaks God's words in faith, God always provides His Spirit in unlimited measure to produce the manifestation of the spoken Word. How encouraging it is to know that a full supply of God's ability to us will back up His own words through us! We can rest assured that when we proclaim God's words, He is determined to produce what He said.

No Limitations to God's Supply of Power

Just think for a moment—were there any limitations to the creation process as God spoke life-filled words? Even Jesus, knowing that the Word carried such power, fulfilled something spoken years before He ever entered into this world when He healed all who were sick and cast demons out with a word. (Matthew 8:16-17.) There was no limitation to those words spoken by the prophet Isaiah. The Spirit of God was in full supply to accomplish the task at hand.

Thank God, His Word has never lost its power! It is just as real today as it was yesterday. Hebrews 13:8 NKJV confirms this truth: **Jesus Christ is the same yesterday, today, and forever.**

As believers, we are entitled to the same supply of the Spirit of God concerning the Word of God as Jesus experienced. Here are some Scriptures that highlight these thoughts even further:

> **And of His fullness we have all received, and grace for grace.**
>
> **John 1:16** NKJV

> **For in Him dwells all the fullness of the Godhead bodily;**
> **And you are complete in Him, who is the head of all principality and power.**
>
> **Colossians 2:9-10** NKJV

> **For it pleased the Father that in him should all fulness dwell.**
>
> **Colossians 1:19**

> **To them God willed to make known what are the riches of the glory of this mystery among the Gentiles: which is Christ in you, the hope of glory.**
>
> **Colossians 1:27** NKJV

But if you give yourself to the Lord, you and Christ are joined together as one person.

1 Corinthians 6:17 TLB

Not that we are sufficient of ourselves to think of anything as being from ourselves, but our sufficiency is from God.

2 Corinthians 3:5 NKJV

These Scriptures all speak plainly concerning God's provision for us as believers. We have been endowed with the Spirit of God even as Jesus was endowed. Indeed, the Lord's command to go into all the world and preach the gospel "with signs following" is obtainable only because God is faithful to supply us with all the power and ability that we need.

THE SPIRIT WITHOUT MEASURE— PART OF OUR INHERITANCE

Remember the words spoken by John the Baptist: **For this one—sent by God—speaks God's words, for God's Spirit is upon him without measure or limit** (John 3:34 TLB). The Spirit without measure is the equipment given to servants to do the work of God. Jesus said that even as the Father had sent Him, so He has sent us (John 20:21).

If the Father sent Jesus to do His will with a full supply of spiritual equipment, why wouldn't He send us out the same way?

It is the will of God for us to continue the ministry of Jesus. But how could we do that if we were limited in our scope of attainment?

It is obvious that Jesus wanted more than one person to be the embodiment of God's presence on the earth. This is why He sent out the twelve disciples and seventy others to preach, teach, and heal in the authority of His name (Luke 10:1). Jesus knew that He was physically limited in the scope of His outreach, for it was impossible for Him to be at all places at the same time.

Jesus had a great compassion for the number of people who needed His touch, as is evident in this passage of Scripture:

> **Then Jesus went about all the cities and villages, teaching in their synagogues, preaching the gospel of the kingdom, and healing every sickness and every disease among the people.**
>
> **But when He saw the multitudes, He was moved with compassion for them, because they were weary and scattered, like sheep having no shepherd.**
>
> **Then He said to His disciples, "The harvest truly is plentiful, but the laborers are few.**

"Therefore pray the Lord of the harvest to send out laborers into His harvest."

And when He had called His twelve disciples to Him, He gave them power over unclean spirits, to cast them out, and to heal all kinds of sickness and all kinds of disease.

Matthew 9:35-38—10:1 NKJV:

Seeing the multitudes, Jesus was moved with compassion. Since He was and always will be the solution for all of man's needs, Jesus's love for the people caused Him to provide a temporary solution to the problem of supply and demand by appointing the twelve disciples to do just as He did.

Notice that Jesus authorized the twelve disciples with sufficient power to heal every sickness and disease and to cast out all unclean spirits. This would lead us to believe that the Spirit without measure is the power and authority necessary to more than adequately accomplish the task at hand. If, on the other hand, we assume that the body of Christ *collectively* has the measure of power and authority that Jesus held *individually*, then we diminish the effectiveness of the continued ministry of Jesus.

Consider this: if Jesus had the Holy Spirit without measure, but we individually have only a portion of the collective measure, then each of us is destined to produce minimal results.

It is the same principle that applies when we divide a pie into twelve pieces. Each piece is only one-twelfth of the whole pie. If Jesus proportionately distributed His anointing in a similar way, each of the disciples would have had only one-twelfth of Jesus's anointing when they were sent out. Only when they came together would they have equaled again the fullness of Christ. Thus, each disciple would only be able to expect one out of every twelve devils to come out and one out of every twelve sicknesses to be healed.

Here is this principle: every time corporate efforts are multiplied, individual effectiveness decreases. Looking from the perspective of the Pauline revelation, we can see that this was definitely not the Lord's intention. Jesus came to multiply Himself.

The Bible says that if Satan had known God's plan, he never would have crucified the Lord of glory. (1 Corinthians 2:8 NKJV.) Isn't the reason obvious? God's plan included making salvation available to the world so that He could have many replicas of the Christ, the Anointed One.

Remember, we are called Christians, which means "just like Christ." We are the devil's worst nightmare. Every time Satan sees a Christian, he is reminded of his horrible defeat by the hand of Jesus Christ. The degree to which a Christian understands his place and calling in light of this truth will determine his effectiveness for God's kingdom in this world.

Limitations are not of God. God has given us complete access to the ministry of Jesus. Every time we believers run up against a difficulty, we are not to question whether we are capable of succeeding. If questions linger and inadequacies settle in, we will be easily defeated. We are to know that we are filled with God, with more than enough of His Spirit and power to meet every demand.

Jesus said in John 10:10, **The thief cometh not, but for to steal, and to kill, and to destroy: I am come that they might have life, and that they might have it more abundantly.** The words "abundance," "sufficiency," and "fullness" are all words that imply *absolute domination.* Believers were never meant to fail. Jesus never failed in His personal life, and He always succeeded in His ministry.

We have the same nature, the same ability, and the same Spirit that filled Jesus. The same eternal life that dwelt within Him is within us as well. That life is our ability to triumph in life and to enjoy the blessing of helping others achieve victory over Satan and his works.

I firmly believe that we usurp the authority of God's Word when we rely on our present status in the natural to determine how much of God we possess. If we are to be biblical in our beliefs, we must acknowledge that the risen Christ and His fullness live within us (Colosians 2:9,10).

Filled with the Spirit, Filled with His Power

Every believer has the potential of living his life like Jesus. This is why the apostle Paul says in Ephesians 5:18, **Be filled with the Spirit,** or as the original language suggests, "Be being filled." In other words, this scripture is saying, "Continually stay filled with the Spirit," or "Be actively participating with the fullness of God within."

We could better understand this concept by seeing our spiritual condition in relation to a bank account. Spiritually, God has generously supplied us with a personal bank account of His blessings. Every spiritual blessing is ours, and a fresh load of benefits is deposited into our account every day. (Psalms 68:19; Ephesians 1:3.) Staying continually filled with the Holy Spirit is like making continual deposits into our account.

So many Christians are spiritually depleted, which makes spiritual success very difficult. The reason is not that God is running a tab on how many spiritual exercises a believer needs to perform to win the prize. After all, God has already won the prize for them. But when believers are out of touch with the Holy Spirit, they are out of touch with the very Source of power needed to produce the results Jesus did by the Spirit.

When we fellowship with God, use our faith, and stir up our spirits with the Word, we are making spiritual deposits into our accounts of the fullness of God. Our supply is very accessible, and our minds are settled and convinced.

When Jesus walked on the earth, He did so as a man. He, the Son of God, became the Son of Man.

Legally, it would have to be so. If Jesus had purchased the redemption of mankind as God, it would have been an illegal intrusion into the world's system, which belonged to the devil. Men were and are being born into the world all the time under the influence of the nature of sin. Therefore, the only legal entrance into the world for the Son of God was as a man—a man without the nature of sin. This Man was then able to assume the role and responsibilities of the first Adam.

First Corinthians 15:45 tells us that Jesus was the last Adam. He was born just as Adam—a perfect human being without sin. If the first Adam could corrupt God's plan as a sinful man, the last Adam could restore God's plan as a sinless Man.

My point is this: is it possible that Jesus walked in the glory and honor in which Adam walked? In other words, could it be that the anointing that came on Jesus after being baptized in the river Jordan was the same anointing that was on the first Adam?

I think it is interesting that Jesus never said before the Cross that the power and authority He possessed was *all* the power and authority that existed in heaven and earth. Yes, Jesus distributed power and authority to the disciples to heal *all* sickness and *all* disease and to cast out *all* devils. However, the emphasis of the *all* in this context was in relationship to the number of healings and deliverances expected.

As Jesus said in Luke 11:20 NKJV, God is able to expel devils with nothing more than His finger: "**But if I cast out demons with the finger of God, surely the kingdom of God has come upon you.**" Since that is true, why was it necessary for Jesus to possess *all* power and authority?

Yes, Jesus was given and walked in the Spirit without measure. But what was God's purpose in giving Him the Spirit without measure? To enable Jesus to accomplish *all* the will of God on the earth as the last Adam.

If this is true, it certainly sheds a different light on our defeated adversary. We discover that we are not struggling so much with the devil as we are with our own inability to see past our insecurities.

Paul told the Corinthians that they were limited by their own affections (2 Corinthians 6:12). It is a common problem for all of us. This natural world's system will distract us from the truth of our victory. That is why John stressed in 1 John 5:4, **This is the victory that overcometh the world** [the world's system and man's self-efforts to obtain status and freedom], **even our faith.** John was talking about faith in the finished work of redemption here—the knowledge that Jesus fought, won, and secured our complete success for life.

If we look further into the life and ministry of Jesus, we see Him in prayer to the Father about the day when redemption would be complete:

> **Jesus spoke these words, lifted up His eyes to heaven, and said: "Father, the hour has come. Glorify Your Son, that Your Son also may glorify You,**
>
> **"As You have given Him authority over all flesh, that He should give eternal life to as many as You have given Him.**
>
> **"And this is eternal life, that they may know You, the only true God, and Jesus Christ whom You have sent.**
>
> **"I have glorified You on the earth. I have finished the work which You have given Me to do.**
>
> **"And now, O Father, glorify Me together with Yourself, with the glory which I had with You before the world was."**
>
> **John 17:1-5 NKJV**

We know that this prayer was prophetically speaking of the day when the penalty of sin would be paid because Jesus was speaking of finishing the work of the Father. The work of the Father was not complete until Jesus ascended with His own blood to secure an eternal redemption for us all. This explains what happened in the garden after Jesus's resurrection, when He told Mary not to touch Him, for He had not yet ascended to His Father to present His blood before Him. (John 20:17; Hebrews 9:7-14.)

Notice in John 17:5 that Jesus prayed, **"Glorify Me with the glory which I had with You before the world was."** This indicates that the divine power He operated in while on the earth was not the fullness of the power He originally possessed. Could this be the reason the apostle Paul wanted to know the power *of His resurrection?* (Philippians 3:10.)

In Ephesians 1:15-20, Paul prayed for the church to be enlightened to the working of God's mighty power, which was demonstrated when He raised Christ from the dead. The greatest recorded work that the Father performed was raising Jesus from the dead. When He raised Jesus, He was raising the whole world. In Christ, the Father reconciled the world to Himself, not imputing their trespasses to them. (2 Corinthians 5:18-19.)

What an awesome display of God's strength and love! The resurrection of Jesus Christ was a demonstration of unmatched power.

Fresh from the grave, Jesus met His disciples:

> And Jesus came and spoke to them, saying, "All authority has been given to Me in heaven and on earth.
>
> "Go therefore and make disciples of all the nations, baptizing them in the name of the Father and of the Son and of the Holy Spirit,
>
> "teaching them to observe all things that I have commanded you; and lo, I am with you always, even to the end of the age." Amen.
>
> **Matthew 28:18-20** NKJV

This is the first time we hear from the lips of Jesus the word "all" used in reference to power and authority. Again, could it be that when the price of sin was paid, the fullness of *all* the glory and power of God raised Jesus from the dead, thus reestablishing to the Christ that which rightfully belonged to Him?

The greatness of God raised Jesus from the dead, and the same Spirit who raised Jesus from the dead is even now quickening our mortal bodies. (Romans 8:11.)

TAKE OFF THE LIMITS!

Think of it, Christian! Bury your insufficiency in the sea of God's grandeur. Never again allow your mind to dishonor the power of the gospel. Forever see your worth and importance in God's plan. Thank God that in His fullness He came to dwell within man, to dwell within you.

For it is God Who is all the while effectually at work in you [energizing and creating in you the power and desire], both to will and to work for His good pleasure and satisfaction and delight.

Philippians 2:13 AMP

This pleasure, satisfaction, and delight—God's perfect will—was set forth by Jesus in Matthew 28:18-20 at the time of His ascension into heaven.

As the body of Christ, we have limited ourselves—which is something Jesus never did. The triumphant church has cowered down before the evil works of Satan. We have drifted so far from the standard of Christianity that we don't recognize the fear and unbelief in which we have embalmed ourselves.

Yet some have blamed God for their lack of results. These are the people who are always asking God to do something more. Thank God for waves of the Spirit, moves of God, and the latter rain. He provides all of that so greater results can be produced to His glory.

However, the purpose of all these wonderful demonstrations is not intended to compensate for what we have not accomplished. The finished work of Christ is enough.

God's plan is sufficient. But it is up to each of us to accomplish that which God has called us to do within that divine plan.

Oh, my fellow believer, hear what the Spirit is saying to the church. Let us rise up and be responsible. Let us consider it an honor to take God at His Word without diluting the power of His message with our own traditional interpretations.

I challenge you: break out of your box. Move beyond the limitations of your mind where reason struggles to reign as king. Cast off the restraints of fear and insecurity.

See yourself in Christ, clothed with His glory. You are a champion—qualified, fortified, and equipped for battle. Not only is it time for you to see your own life enhanced; it is also time for you to be able to set someone else free!

Chapter 8

YOU ARE A GIFT— HOW THE GIFTS OF THE SPIRIT OPERATE

I n the midst of a chaotic world that judges worth based on performance, Jesus inspired Peter to write and remind us that when we were nothing, God made us something special.

> But you are not like that, for you have been chosen by God himself—you are priests of the King, you are holy and pure, you are God's very own—all this so that you may show to others how God called you out of the darkness into his wonderful light.
>
> Once you were less than nothing; now you are

God's own. Once you knew very little of God's kindness; now your very lives have been changed by it.

1 Peter 2:9-10 TLB

We have been chosen by God. This fact alone should inspire within us a sense of destined greatness. The God of the universe has chosen us, called us, and equipped us to be victorious. We are His very own. Holy and pure is the way He made us; righteous and blessed is the way we stand before Him.

How can sin steal our self-worth? Is it more powerful than the kindness of God? Oh, how our Father longs for us to view ourselves through His eyes!

CONFIDENCE IN WHAT YOU HAVE IN HIM

We will endeavor to stay focused throughout this study, always mindful that the ministry of Jesus was marked by His understanding of destiny. He not only knew where He came from; He also understood the purpose for each day that He lived on this earth.

Turning our attention to the fourth chapter of John, let's discover what Jesus knew:

So He came to a city of Samaria which is called Sychar, near the plot of ground that Jacob gave to his son Joseph.

Now Jacob's well was there. Jesus therefore, being wearied from His journey, sat thus by the well. It was about the sixth hour.

A woman of Samaria came to draw water. Jesus said to her, "Give Me a drink."

For His disciples had gone away into the city to buy food.

Then the woman of Samaria said to Him, "How is it that You, being a Jew, ask a drink from me, a Samaritan woman?" For Jews have no dealings with Samaritans.

Jesus answered and said to her, "If you knew the gift of God, and who it is who says to you, 'Give Me a drink,' you would have asked Him, and He would have given you living water."

John 4:5-10 NKJV

As we can see from verses 6 and 7, Jesus was tired and thirsty from His journey. But when Jesus asked the Samaritan woman for a drink, the woman was shocked. Her response in verse 9 was typical, though, considering the tension between the Samaritans and the Jews. These two tribes of people despised one another. If there were any dealings at all between Jews and Samaritans, it was strictly business. Certainly there were no acts of kindness.

I like what Jesus did at this point. He turned the entire

conversation into an opportunity for personal ministry. Jesus began by saying, "If you knew..."

It is amazing to me how much we miss as Christians because of what we don't know. If the woman had known who Jesus was, she could have received the benefits of knowing. She also could have received those benefits because of what Jesus knew.

Knowing is important for the giver so the gift can be given. It is also important for the recipient so the gift can be received.

There are four things Jesus knew.

1. Jesus knew He was a gift of God. As John 3:16 says, **For God so loved the world, that he gave his only begotten Son.**
2. Jesus knew who He was. Everywhere He went, He would read from the prophet Isaiah saying, "The Spirit of the Lord is upon Me for He has anointed Me." (See Isaiah 61:1.) Jesus knew He was the answer for the world.
3. Jesus knew He had living water (John 4:10). What a tremendous revelation this is! Are you confident that you possess the life and nature of God? *Knowing* that you have life is half the key to releasing it.
4. Jesus knew that when asked, He could give this living water (John 4:13-14).

In John 5:26 NKJV, Jesus said, **"For as the Father has life in Himself, so He has granted the Son to have life in Himself."** Ultimately, it was Jesus who came that we might have life.

In John 10:10, Jesus said, **I am come that they might have life, and that they might have it more abundantly.** Jesus reemphasized this truth in John 4:14 NKJV:

> **"But whoever drinks of the water that I shall give him will never thirst. But the water that I shall give him will become in him a fountain of water springing up into everlasting life."**

It is very plain to see the confidence Jesus had in what He possessed in God and in His ability to give it away.

It is necessary to see the significance of what Jesus was saying and doing before we move on to the next point. For a moment, let me refresh your memory regarding the different facets of Jesus's ministry.

There is a man side, which focuses on the faith of the individual receiving from God. There is also a God side, which is God through the gifts of the Spirit initiating a blessing toward man. And, finally, there is the God-man side, which places responsibility on the person who is ministering to use his anointing and faith to help someone who is having trouble releasing his own faith.

As we discovered in the ministry of Jesus, the third

method, or the God-man side, was the most common way Jesus operated when dealing with people individually. It is also the reason so many people followed Him. As Jesus demonstrated His ability to get results, people believed in Him.

Anyone in business can appreciate this thought. When a person is successful at what he does, people will spread the word and his business will grow. If Christianity had always produced results like those produced by Jesus and the early church, there would be no room left for all the other religions in the world.

Now let's consider again what Jesus said and did in John 4. He was extremely aware and confident about what He had and His ability to do something with it. He proclaimed that He was a gift. He knew who He was, and He knew He possessed living water that He could give away and bring blessing to the recipient.

Jesus took an active role in pursuit of this woman's faith. He didn't seem to be cautious about His ability to produce results. He was confident about what He had and what it would do for her.

Confidence in What God Has Made You to Be

As discussed earlier, the active role of the deliverer or mediator will bring the God side and the man side together. When a deliverer is bold about what God will do and confident in the ability with which God has entrusted him, he will always be able to produce more faith in people and there will always be more gifts of the Spirit in operation in their lives.

In His encounter with the Samaritan woman, Jesus didn't wait for a gift of the Spirit to produce something; He knew that *He* was a gift. He believed in the living water He possessed, and He knew it would bring blessing to this woman.

God will always work with a doer. What kind of doer am I talking about? He works with the person who steps out in faith and obeys when given a particular purpose or assignment in the earth. Whatever God's will is for that person's life, whatever equipment He has entrusted him with in order to complete the task, the doer is faithful to use what he has to do the works of Jesus and produce the desired results.

In Acts 10:38 NKJV, Peter preached, **"God anointed Jesus of Nazareth with the Holy Spirit and with power, who went about doing good and healing all who were oppressed by the devil, for God was with Him."** The *purpose* was to do good and to heal all who were oppressed by the devil. The *empowerment* to accomplish the purpose was the Holy Spirit and power.

Jesus was very confident of the Father's abiding presence because He was faithful to exercise His right to perform the will of God that He had been sent to do.

If God has commanded you to fulfill a particular mission, He has given you the ability to perform it. Therefore, the only way you can be intimidated about the outcome is by questioning the integrity of God and your ability to perform—which is unbelief and fear of failure. Never forget—God will *never* ask you to do anything for which He will not equip you with the ability to complete the task successfully.

RELY ON JESUS FOR THE RESULTS, NOT ON MAN'S EFFORTS

Jesus's next step in helping this woman is most interesting. In John 4:15 NKJV, she said to Jesus, **"Sir, give me this water."** Jesus had obviously produced a great desire in her to receive.

Look at Jesus's response to her: **"Go, call your husband, and come here"** (v. 16 NKJV). At a time when it didn't seem as though Jesus needed any help in what He was doing, a gift of the Spirit began to operate. Jesus received a word of knowledge—insight into her past or present. God worked with Jesus to complete what Jesus had started in ministering to this Samaritan woman.

This spiritual gift was obviously necessary for the situation. It certainly revealed something hidden that would have hindered this woman's ability to receive.

But my point is this: Jesus relied not on the gift but on

who He was and what He possessed to help this woman. As we will see through the following illustration, Jesus never made the church conscious of the fact that a gift of the Spirit was needed to cause an instantaneous result. On the contrary, Jesus spent His time developing in His followers a consciousness of results based on (1) what He said the church possesses and (2) on what He said the church can do with that spiritual equipment.

Before we get to the illustration, let's discuss for a moment the gifts of the Spirit. We mentioned these gifts in chapter 2; however, let's review them again:

> But the manifestation of the Spirit is given to each one for the profit of all:
>
> for to one is given the word of wisdom through the Spirit, to another the word of knowledge through the same Spirit,
>
> to another faith by the same Spirit, to another gifts of healings by the same Spirit,
>
> to another the working of miracles, to another prophecy, to another discerning of spirits, to another different kinds of tongues, to another the interpretation of tongues.
>
> But one and the same Spirit works all these things, distributing to each one individually as He wills.
>
> 1 Corinthians 12:7-11 NKJV

As the church, we ought to be thankful that the Lord in His goodness has provided special manifestations for believers. These gifts are part of the equipment for the church to do its job in the earth.

Faith in God will produce anything that a gift of the Spirit will produce. Thus, the primary emphasis for Christians is to walk in faith according to their redemption. However, God will use gifts in the church to meet needs and help believers in their walk with Him.

When David talked to Goliath, the young man spoke some very profound words. David said that for two reasons he would kill Goliath: (1) So all the world would know that God lived in Israel; and (2) So all of Israel would know that God's people did not fight with sword and spear, for the battle is the Lord's (1 Samuel 17:46-47).

When the people of God get so far away from the truth, it is easy to lose perspective. The standard is always Jesus. Yet so many are content if they are doing a little better than the Joneses.

God will use signs and wonders as a wake-up call to the church. Yet the real purpose for the gifts of the Spirit is to minister to the world.

It is important to realize, however, that the Spirit manifests gifts as He wills. (1 Corinthians 12:11.) This realization makes this statement crucial, for it is the understanding that the Holy Spirit is very willing to move on our behalf. We should therefore always be on the side of believing Him to do more rather than do less. I say this knowing it becomes very difficult to expect God to work with us concerning the gifts when we see so little of them in operation.

Perhaps this is why the apostle Paul started the twelfth chapter of 1 Corinthians by saying, he didn't want the Corinthians to be ignorant of spiritual things or things pertaining to the Holy Ghost.

One way to be ignorant of spiritual things is not to know how to correctly operate in the gifts of the Spirit. We must always consider others and walk in love to facilitate the gifts of the Spirit. We will only get in trouble if we are motivated by the flesh or if we yield to wrong spirits by trying to make things happen in our own strength. This is a dangerous temptation when we are being pressured to produce results. It is always better to keep our emphasis on faith in the Word for results rather than to push for spectacular demonstrations in the Spirit.

Let me add a thought here. In one sense, we could say that the Holy Spirit is always willing. Even though this may sound exaggerated, it really has merit when we look at 1 Corinthians 12:11. If the Holy Spirit doesn't see a need for a gift of the Spirit, He is always willing to respond to faith by manifesting His power. This willingness on His part encompasses everything we could ever need in life.

God will meet our faith by moving on our behalf in response to our prayers, or He will move on our behalf through a spiritual gift that is independent of us. Either way, He is ready and willing to accomplish His will in our lives.

On the other hand, we may be ignorant of the fact that spiritual things are available to us. In that case, we could miss what the Holy Spirit wants to do in our lives.

But we can also decide to stay right in the middle and, through our relationship with God, come to understand the spirit realm. We can be accurate and ready to move with the Holy Spirit when He moves. It will be the Holy Spirit who does the moving, but He is more than willing to do what He has promised to do.

Replicates of Jesus

In Matthew's Gospel, we see that Jesus gave the disciples power over unclean spirits and power to heal all sickness and disease.

> **And when He had called His twelve disciples to Him, He gave them power over unclean spirits, to cast them out, and to heal all kinds of sickness and all kinds of disease.**
>
> **Matthew 10:1 NKJV**

In the Gospel of Luke, we also see that Jesus gave the disciples power and authority over all devils.

> **Then he called his twelve disciples together, and gave them power and authority over all devils, and to cure diseases.**
>
> **Luke 9:1 KJV**

If we put the two verses together, we see that Jesus gave the disciples power and authority to cast out all devils and to cure all sickness and all disease.

Jesus actually intended for the disciples to overcome every devil and every disease. He replicated His ministry many times over, exactly as if He were doing it Himself.

This message was distributed to eighty-two people— first to the twelve disciples and then to another seventy as well. Think of it—before Jesus ever paid the price of redemption, eighty-two people were casting out every devil and healing every disease!

We only have record of one devil that gave the disciples trouble, and Jesus made the needed correction in that case (Matthew 17:14-21). Therefore, it is safe to say that what Jesus sent His disciples to do was successful. He wouldn't have sent out seventy others if the first twelve had been unsuccessful. Besides, Jesus spent more time with the twelve than with the seventy. If the twelve hadn't produced results, the seventy wouldn't have been expected to produce anything either.

Yet we know that the seventy returned rejoicing that the devils were subject to them in the name of Jesus.

(Luke 10:17-20.) They obviously were successful as they endeavored to do the works of Jesus according to their Master's instructions.

NEVER GIVE UP

Here is a side thought worth noting: Jesus rebuked the twelve about their failure to heal the epileptic boy brought to them. We find this account in Mark 9:17-29:

> And one of the multitude answered and said, Master, I have brought unto thee my son, which hath a dumb spirit;
>
> And wheresoever he taketh him, he teareth him: and he foameth, and gnasheth with his teeth, and pineth away: and I spake to thy disciples that they should cast him out; and they could not.
>
> He answereth him, and saith, O faithless generation, how long shall I be with you? how long shall I suffer you? bring him unto me.
>
> And they brought him unto him: and when he saw him, straightway the spirit tare him; and he fell on the ground, and wallowed foaming.
>
> And he asked his father, How long is it ago since this came unto him? And he said, Of a child.

And ofttimes it hath cast him into the fire, and into the waters, to destroy him: but if thou canst do any thing, have compassion on us, and help us.

Jesus said unto him, If thou canst believe, all things are possible to him that believeth.

And straightway the father of the child cried out, and said with tears, Lord, I believe; help thou mine unbelief.

When Jesus saw that the people came running together, he rebuked the foul spirit, saying unto him, Thou dumb and deaf spirit, I charge thee, come out of him, and enter no more into him.

And the spirit cried, and rent him sore, and came out of him: and he was as one dead; insomuch that many said, He is dead.

But Jesus took him by the hand, and lifted him up; and he arose.

And when he was come into the house, his disciples asked him privately, Why could not we cast him out?

And he said unto them, This kind can come forth by nothing, but by prayer and fasting.

The disciples didn't fail in performing this exorcism because they were initially in unbelief. By this time, they were already very skilled in casting out every kind of devil. Therefore, Jesus didn't rebuke them for failing, but for giving up. If you remember, Jesus said they had authority over *all* devils. He expected them to cast out *every* devil they ever encountered.

We can learn something further from the ministry of Jesus by examining how He dealt with the devil in the madman of the Gadarenes (Mark 5:1-18). Jesus had told the devil to come out of the madman, but it still remained. We don't have record that it even fazed Jesus when the devil did not come out at His first command. We do, however, see Jesus do something that He did nowhere else: He asked the devil its name.

This seems odd to our conventional ways. We were never instructed to talk to devils except to cast them out. This entire scene explains why Jesus told the disciples that prayer and fasting is the only way to get this kind of demon out of a person.

You see, praying and fasting doesn't change *God*; it changes *us*. The more real spiritual things are to us, the easier it is for us to yield to them.

It is obvious that Jesus was being led by the Holy Ghost to ask the devil what its name was. It surely worked. Immediately Jesus had command of the legions of devils inhabiting the madman of Gadara.

The disciples should have allowed God to lead them in knowing what to do to expel the devil out of the boy. Their unbelief was seen only by their giving up. This, however, is the only rebuke recorded concerning the ministry of the disciples as directed by Jesus. They definitely did a great job fulfilling the assignment Jesus had entrusted to them.

ANOINTING-CONSCIOUS VS. GIFT-CONSCIOUS

Let's look further at the specific command Jesus gave the disciples. In Matthew 10:7-8 NKJV, He said:

> "And as you go, preach, saying, 'The kingdom of heaven is at hand.'
> "Heal the sick, cleanse the lepers, raise the dead, cast out demons. Freely you have received, freely give."

When Jesus gave them this command, did you notice what He *didn't* say? Maybe I should phrase my point a different way. Who was the man used by God to bring the revelation of the gifts of the Spirit into the world? Was it Jesus?

Isn't it interesting that Jesus never said anything about the gifts of the Spirit? *Paul* was the one who did that in 1 Corinthians 12:7-11, where he discussed the operations of the gifts. Why did Paul do that? Was it because the Corinthian church didn't know anything about the gifts? Not according to this passage in Paul's first epistle to the Corinthians:

I thank my God always concerning you for the grace of God which was given to you by Christ Jesus,

That you were enriched in everything by Him in all utterance and all knowledge,

Even as the testimony of Christ was confirmed in you,

So that you come short in no gift, eagerly waiting for the revelation of our Lord Jesus Christ,

Who will also confirm you to the end, that you may be blameless in the day of our Lord Jesus Christ.

1 Corinthians 1:4-8 NKJV

We can see that the Corinthian church excelled in the gifts of the Spirit more than any other church. Paul brought up the subject to bring correction and encouragement concerning the operations of the gifts. This is why chapter 13 is written about love. The chapter not only describes what love is, but it is also a reminder that love is the best way to be led by the Holy Spirit.

It is interesting that Paul only spoke once concerning the gifts of the Spirit. Why didn't he talk to every church about it, as he did the realities of redemption or the need to continue in the faith instead of returning to legalism? Why would Paul concentrate more on the power of the love walk or the importance of marital and brotherly kindness?

The list goes on and on. There are many things the apostle Paul spoke about often, but the gifts of the Spirit are rarely mentioned.

Now let's go back to the ministry of Jesus. Jesus didn't share information concerning the gifts of the Spirit, yet He was very specific in His directions to produce results. Jesus told the disciples to heal the sick, cleanse the lepers, and raise the dead.

Those who have studied well the gifts of the Spirit will tell you that it definitely takes gifts to cleanse a leper and raise the dead. Most likely the working of miracles is necessary for the cleansing of lepers, and the three power gifts—special faith, the working of miracles, and the gifts of healing—are necessary to raise the dead.

Why then, didn't Jesus tell the disciples about this spiritual equipment? Because Jesus placed more emphasis on what the disciples had and what they could do with it. He helped them to be *anointing-conscious* and not *gift-conscious.*

A MINISTRY OF RESULTS

When we classify cases needing a miracle according to the gifts that are necessary to deal with them, we disqualify ourselves. Immediately reason steps in to rationalize why we are not able to do what needs to be done.

Perhaps we haven't seen many gifts of the Spirit in manifestation lately, so we are not sure whether God will work with us. We will especially be in trouble if we think that we need gifts in order to see instant manifestations. This attitude will immediately disqualify us from successfully doing what we have specifically been told to do.

So what are we to do? Are we to keep teaching people the Word, trusting that sooner or later they will get it? I can't think of anything better to do if we don't know the next step to take. However, Jesus already told us what to do. He said to *heal the sick*—and He meant *you* heal the sick.

We as the church have drifted so far from the standard of Jesus that we don't recognize our unbelief and our reliance on tradition. We judge our ministries based on someone else's ministry rather than on the ministry of Jesus. When we look honestly at the life and ministry of Jesus, we must hang our heads in shame and repent of our lack of faith and boldness.

If you had been a disciple of Jesus, you would have been privileged to see Jesus never fail or make a mistake concerning anything. When people believed in Him, He always produced results.

Imagine what it would have been like if this were the

only ministry environment you were used to. Then one day Jesus suddenly said to you, "I am giving you the ability to cast out every devil and heal every sickness." How would you have received that news? With great excitement, I am sure.

Jesus reminded the disciples that they had freely received; now He told them that they were to freely *give*. This revelation stuck with them for the rest of their lives.

In Acts 3:1-10, we see Peter operating in this revelation along with the apostle John. Peter said to the crippled man at the door of the temple, "Such as I have, I give you; in the name of Jesus, rise and walk!" And the crippled man not only walked, but went around the temple, walking and leaping and praising God for his healing!

Jesus's ministry of results continued to live on through the apostles as they did the works of their Master. But it was never supposed to stop there. The ministry of the Word and the power of the Spirit should still live on today through us!

Believe That You're Anointed

In the midst of Jesus's successful ministry, He gave the disciples a revelation of the anointing. They were sure they had something because what they received had worked for

Jesus every time. Therefore, why wouldn't it work for them—especially if the Master said it would?

But if Jesus had explained to them all that would be involved in the ministry of healing and miracles, they might have backed off from their bold and confident belief. Can you imagine Peter and John walking up to a leper, wondering whether the right gift would be available for them to heal him?

If that had happened, they would have talked themselves out of healing that man for the same reason we talk ourselves out of healing people today. The realm of reason would have convinced them that they were not equipped enough, that they didn't have enough of the Holy Ghost, or that they hadn't prayed enough or fasted enough to be used in the gifts of the Spirit.

Does that sound familiar? Don't you wish you could truthfully answer no?

We must believe that we are anointed, that the price Jesus paid was enough, and that the work He accomplished was complete. We are His "clones"—made in His image and capable of doing the same work He did. When will we believe it? When we see it?

Be daring, believer! Believe the Bible. Don't get caught in the mind games of the religious, for tradition will rob you blind.

No wonder the devil comes to steal, kill, and destroy. He doesn't want the church to see its potential.

"Put it off," he whispers to your mind. "Get full of the Holy Ghost. Work harder. You're not ready yet. The most spiritual people of the day aren't doing much, so why should you think *you* can do anything? What you need is a great wave of the Spirit. Wait for it. Pray about it. But don't be silly enough to think that anything significant will happen in the meantime."

Don't lose heart, my friend. Remember, Jesus came to give you life, and that more abundantly.

The answer of the ages is the mystery of the ages: Christ in you, the hope of glory. The work is finished. When it comes to your life, the devil is finished and the victory is won. The battle has been fought, and you remain standing while the hosts of darkness lie at your feet.

Throughout the ages the song will be sung, "Holy, Holy, Holy is the Lord God Almighty, Who was, Who is, and Who is to come. Amen." (See Revelation 4:8.)

Will you dare to take your place and believe yourself to be a gift from heaven? Will you endeavor with all your strength to know who you are in Christ and that you possess living water? Will you remain confident that you can give what you have to those who are bound? Will you step forward, knowing that you have something to give?

What will you believe? Whom will you obey?

There is One who from time eternal stands above all. He awaits your decision. Go ahead. You can trust Him.

The world itself spins on His axis. If He said you are, then you are. If He said you have, then you have. If He said you can, then you can. The sum total of your thoughts will be your experience tomorrow.

You are anointed! Dare to believe it!

Chapter 9

GOD IS ALWAYS WORKING

Isn't it comforting to know that God doesn't need any help staying awake? There is no shift work in heaven. God is on alert all the time, ever ready to defend and protect. He never tires and never becomes weary.

I will lift up my eyes to the hills—from whence comes my help?

My help comes from the LORD, who made heaven and earth.

He will not allow your foot to be moved; He who keeps you will not slumber.

Behold, He who keeps Israel shall neither slumber nor sleep.

The LORD is your keeper; the LORD is your shade at your right hand.

The sun shall not strike you by day, nor the moon by night.

The LORD shall preserve you from all evil; He shall preserve your soul.

The LORD shall preserve your going out and your coming in from this time forth, and even forevermore.

Psalm 121:1-8 NKJV

Every minute of every day, He is actively pursuing the fulfillment of His covenant and will on the earth:

"For the eyes of the LORD run to and fro throughout the whole earth, to show Himself strong on behalf of those whose heart is loyal to Him."

2 Chronicles 16:9 NKJV

If God could accomplish His plans and purposes all by Himself, He would have done so long ago. Notice in this verse that He is searching for a loyal, trustworthy soul who believes He is more than enough. This is the kind of individual He can work through.

The context of this verse is surrounded by the lack of trust King Asa of Judah displayed before God. Earlier when the Ethiopians and the Lubim had attacked him, Asa had put his trust in God. At that time God delivered Judah from the hands of their enemies, even though the enemy's army was much bigger.

But at this moment, another enemy has come to threaten Judah, and the prophet Hanani is rebuking Asa for relying on the King of Syria instead of on God. This is when the prophet says that the eyes of the Lord roam throughout the whole earth in search of a loyal heart so that He might show Himself strong on his behalf.

God seems to be anticipating someone who will trust Him wholeheartedly. He also seems to be very ready to accommodate faith with a great response of strength.

Moving the Immovable on Your Behalf

What would it look like for the Lord to move strongly on *your* behalf?

In John 3, as Jesus talked with Nicodemus about spiritual things, He was compelled to use natural understanding to help him comprehend spiritual truths. For instance, when describing the Holy Ghost and the work of the Spirit, He used the wind as a parallel saying that the wind moves, yet you don't see it unless you see what it moves; so it is with the Spirit (v. 8).

If we were to look outside and determine the strength

of the wind, it would be in relation to what the wind was moving. If we said, "There is just a light breeze," we would be describing the leaves that were barely moving or the grass that was gently blowing.

On the other hand, if we were describing a strong wind, we would relate it to something that is ordinarily immovable but that is now moving. For instance, if a big tree were to get blown over, we would say, "That was a *strong* wind!"

Now relate that illustration to your walk with the Lord. If God were moving strongly on your behalf, what kind of immovable things would He move out of your life? How about cancer, or oppression, or financial despair? In the midst of battle, these obstacles certainly seem immovable at times.

But how often does the Lord *want* to work on your behalf? As often as you let Him and as long as there are objects to move.

One Man's Deliverance Despite Doubt

Jesus said similar things in John 5. Here we see the account of the paralyzed man at the Pool of Bethesda. Surrounding this pool were five porches full of sick people, waiting for an angel of the Lord to come down and stir the water. When the water was stirred, the first one in would be healed of whatever illness he had.

It is interesting to note that the sick who populated the porches surrounding the pool seem to have chosen their method of deliverance. They were waiting to see something before they would believe and act. Perhaps this is the reason Jesus didn't go to any other sick person on the five porches. Certainly He knew that it is very difficult to move someone into faith when that individual doesn't want help.

So what was the difference with the man Jesus healed? Jesus was *led* to go to him. Any one of the sick people could have had someone take him or her to one of Jesus's meetings. However, they had chosen their method of healing. In that sense, the stirring of the waters represent a lack of faith and a need for the natural senses in order to believe.

This sounds like the church today. Many Christians have the right confession about their healing, but they are still waiting for their symptoms to change before they will believe that they receive.

As Jesus approached the man lying at the pool, the Holy Spirit gave Him a word of knowledge concerning the man's situation. Jesus knew the man had been in that condition for thirty-eight years, a very long time. So He asked the man, **"Do you want to be made well?"** (v. 6 NKJV).

The man's response reveals his lack of faith: **"Sir, I have no man to put me into the pool when the water is stirred up; but while I am coming, another steps down before me."** (v. 7).

This account is very different from that of blind Bartimaeus, who responded with excitement toward the Lord. The man at the Pool of Bethesda didn't know it was Jesus who was talking with him.

As I mentioned in an earlier chapter, there were gifts of the Spirit operating in this situation. The man was healed without even believing in Jesus as his healer. Certainly he had to obey the command of Jesus, but how difficult was that command? His legs received strength before he even stood up. Anyone can be healed when healing takes place on its own. Thus, it is evident that faith was not exercised here.

WORKING WITH THE GOD WHO IS ALWAYS WORKING

Afterwards, as Jesus presented Himself to the man, the man placed his faith in Him. Let's read what happened at this point:

> For this reason the Jews persecuted Jesus, and sought to kill Him, because He had done these things on the Sabbath.
>
> But Jesus answered them, "My Father has been working until now, and I have been working."

Therefore the Jews sought all the more to kill Him, because He not only broke the Sabbath, but also said that God was His Father, making Himself equal with God.

Then Jesus answered and said to them, "Most assuredly, I say to you, the Son can do nothing of Himself, but what He sees the Father do; for whatever He does, the Son also does in like manner.

"For the Father loves the Son, and shows Him all things that He Himself does; and He will show Him greater works than these, that you may marvel.

"For as the Father raises the dead and gives life to them, even so the Son gives life to whom He will."

John 5:16-21 NKJV

Verse 16 describes a situation Jesus often encountered, since He would often produce miracles on the Sabbath. In this case, the Jews sought to kill Him because of this very thing. Jesus responded in verse 17 by saying, **"My Father has been working until now, and I have been working."**

The New International Version of the Bible says, **"My Father is always at his work to this very day, and I, too,** am working." The Living Bible says, "**My Father constantly does good, and I'm following his example.**"

This passage complements the Scriptures we read at the beginning of this chapter. But if our Father is always at work, why aren't we seeing more evidence in our lives and ministries of what He is working on?

Notice the following phrase: "**I, too, am working**" (v. 17 NIV). This indicates that there is a connection between the Father and the Son working together. Is it possible that a similar connection exists between the Father and the church as well?

This is a good question to ask, since we in the church are so often waiting for God to move before we dare to move. Jesus said that the Father is working all the time. What then would hinder the manifest presence of God in any situation other than fear and a lack of initiative on our part?

PERSISTENT FAITH IS REWARDED WITH RESULTS

I have personally experienced many results in my ministry just by believing that God is always working. My part is to work with Him as I maintain the same testimony Enoch was known for: that he always pleased God.

> **By faith Enoch was translated that he should
> not see death, and was not found, because God**

**had translated him: for before his translation he
had this testimony, that he pleased God.**

Hebrews 11:5

What made the intimate relationship between God
and Enoch possible? First, it was Enoch's belief that God
is. Hebrews 11:6 follows the reference to Enoch's walk
with God, telling us that, **without faith it is impossible to
please him: for he that cometh to God must believe that
he is, and that he is a rewarded of them that diligently
seek him.**

Notice the word "must." It is a "must" that first and foremost we believe that God is. Relating this point to our discussion, we must believe that God is always working, which
gives us the right to work with Him and expect results.

The rest of verse 6 says that when we diligently seek
God, He will reward us. Or we could put it this way: If we
are persistent in believing what God has said, we will be
rewarded with results. For instance, Jesus stated that when
believers lay hands on the sick, the sick will recover (Mark
16:18). Our part is to believe that this is what happens,
regardless of how the situation seems in the natural.

I have had many experiences in which persistence has
brought the manifestation of healing. One case in particular
that I remember took place in healing school.

A woman attending the service had cancer in her
breast. She could actually feel the tumor. I ministered to

her and sent her out to check the area that was infected. When she returned, she was very excited, for the tumor had shrunk to half its former size.

I said to her, "You won't go out two more times without it being gone." That was the command of faith. I declared it to give the woman something to believe in.

When the woman returned the second time, she testified that the area where the tumor was located felt hot and that she could feel God's power working. I rejoiced with her. Then I reminded her of what I had said earlier: She would not go out two more times without the tumor being gone.

I finally sent her out for the last time. As she walked back into the room, I noticed that the expression on her face was saying the tumor hadn't left. So I made a big "to-do" about the miracle lady, exclaiming how excited we all were to receive her testimony.

The woman walked halfway down the aisle. Then she stopped to report that although the area was very hot, the tumor was still there.

I wanted to make an impression on the rest of the people, so I came off the platform, walked up to her, and shouted, "I don't believe that. The Word can't fail."

She looked astonished and said slowly, "Well, well, it's still there."

I persisted: "Did you hear what I said earlier? I said that after two more times of checking, the tumor would disappear. And that's exactly what happened!"

She looked around, then she looked back at me and began to stutter again. I stopped her and said again, "I *said* you wouldn't go out two more times without it disappearing. Do you understand that?"

Suddenly, the light went on in her. I could see it in her eyes. Her whole countenance changed.

She said, "Yes, I do. I believe it *is* gone."

She then spun around to go to the back of the room and check it once more. When she did, the rest of the tumor had disappeared. Glory to God!

When she went to the doctor, his report simply corroborated what the woman already knew. God confirmed His Word and she was completely healed.

DUPLICATING JESUS'S RESULTS ON THIS EARTH

Jesus said that His Father is always working. Someone may say, "But what happens if the healing is not instantaneous?" Thank God for faith! That is why we believe that we receive. Faith considers the answer before it sees it and rejoices as though the manifestation of the answer is already complete—because it *is*.

However, something we must all strive for is attaining the percentage of success Jesus enjoyed when He ministered to the sick. Jesus healed the sick instantly the majority of the time. For us to be satisfied with anything less would be to fall short of what Jesus told us in John 14:12 NKJV:

> "**Most assuredly, I say to you, he who believes in Me, the works that I do he will do also; and greater works than these he will do, because I go to My Father.**"

Nowhere did Jesus tell us or leave us with the idea that when we work the works of God, we will experience different results than He did. On the contrary, He told us that each member of the body of Christ is expected to duplicate His results as we minister to a lost world.

It is Jesus's desire to lift us out of ourselves and our insufficiency and to create in us a strength of purpose. No believer should ever question whether the power of God will work the same in his or her life as it did in the life of Christ. After all, the life, nature, and power of God were given to the church for that very purpose!

God's desire for mankind is not just to get them saved. He has a higher purpose. God is creating a new species of people called Christians—men and women filled with the same ability as their elder Brother Jesus possessed and called to finish the work He started.

This is the reason the devil would never have crucified the Lord of glory (1 Corinthians 2:18) if he had understood God's plan of redemption. The enemy didn't understand until it was too late that believers would be empowered and equipped with the exact same power and ability that raised Jesus from the dead.

God started a new species of people when He raised up Jesus. As members of that new species, we are not just *capable* of doing the works of Jesus—we are *commanded* to do the works of Jesus.

ALWAYS VICTORY, NEVER DEFEAT

Look again at the words of Jesus in John 5:17 NIV: "**My Father is always at his work this very day, and I, too, am working.**" Philippians 2:13 AMP confirms this truth that God is always working:

> **It is God Who is all the while effectually at work in you [energizing and creating in you the power and desire], both to will and to work for His good pleasure and satisfaction and delight.**

What else do we know about the word "always"?

- We know that Jesus will never leave us nor forsake us (Hebrews 13:5); therefore, He is *always* with us.
- We know that we *always* have all sufficiency in

all things (2 Corinthians 9:8).

- We know that we *always* triumph in Christ Jesus (2 Corinthians 2:14).

Given these great promises, what room is left for failure? Jesus never approached a situation wondering whether He could do the works of His Father. He never said, "I hope what I'm about to do doesn't fail."

Always, even in His own hometown, Jesus was the picture of absoluteness. Even in the midst of unbelief, He still wanted to do mighty works, although the Bible says at times He couldn't do them because of the people's lack of faith (Matthew 13:53-58).

Jesus never stopped for one moment to consider what might not happen. His soul knew only victory, success, and the right to dominate the works of the devil. There wasn't the smallest ounce of failure in Him. He accepted His divine purpose—spirit, soul, and body. And with His disciples, He rebuked the slightest unbelief.

Was Jesus too expectant? Was He too demanding? No, He just understood what it takes to succeed in God.

You Have the Mind of Christ

Before we leave this chapter, let's look at John 5:18-21 in the NKJV:

Therefore the Jews sought all the more to kill Him, because He not only broke the Sabbath, but also said that God was His Father, making Himself equal with God.

Then Jesus answered and said to them, "Most assuredly, I say to you, the Son can do nothing of Himself, but what He sees the Father do; for whatever He does, the Son also does in like manner.

"For the Father loves the Son, and shows Him all things that He Himself does; and He will show Him greater works than these, that you may marvel.

"For as the Father raises the dead and gives life to them, even so the Son gives life to whom He will."

In this passage, Jesus revealed keys to our success as His apprentices in ministry. For instance, in verse 19, He said that everything He did was that which He saw the Father do.

This may sound a little intimidating as we are developing our relationship with the Lord. We may wonder whether we see God at all. But Jesus gave us the key in verse 20: **"For the Father loves the Son..."**

How much does the Father love you? In John 17, Jesus said that just as the Father has loved Him, so He loves you.

Let's finish the thought in the rest of verse 20, **"and shows Him all things that He Himself does."** Notice in verses 20 and 21 how emphatically Jesus spoke about things that hadn't even come to pass yet. This, my friend, is Faith 101. Jesus was demonstrating how to move into the realm of the Spirit with faith. As we follow His lead and begin to think like He thinks, you and I will also be able to say with confidence, "Because the Father loves me, He shows me all things that He Himself does."

Later Jesus said that this was one of the purposes the Holy Ghost would come to indwell our hearts—to show us things to come (John 16:13).

Are you waiting for this to happen? If you are, then you will always wait for it. You must rather accept this divine promise as truth and begin to confess it. Allow it to become yours by acting as though it is true. As you do, you will discover that God will not let you down.

Notice that Jesus didn't stop in verse 20. He went on to say that God would show Him greater works than these **"that you may marvel."**

I realize that you may be marveling right now that Jesus's words could work for you, too. But remember, Jesus did everything He did as a man.

Of course, Jesus didn't have to unlearn the negative thoughts we know so well. However, when it came time to learn the positive realities of God His Father, He did so just as we must do. Jesus developed in His walk with God through the Word, prayer, fellowship, and a conscious choice to believe without question the words of His Father.

In First Corinthians 2:16, Paul said that we have the mind of Christ; therefore, it is possible to have it. I encourage you to believe that all things are possible with you. Dare to see yourself in an intimate relationship with God. Confidently expect to hear His voice and see His works demonstrated in your life.

God has provided you with a written account of what Jesus did when He walked on this earth. So why not imitate the Master? Someday will never come—why not make *today* the day when things change with you?

Your faith is real, God is real, and your ability to make the right decision will move the impossible to possible!

Chapter 10

IN HIS IMAGE

Then God said, "Let us make a man—
someone like ourselves, to be the master of all life
upon the earth and in the skies and in the seas."

So God made man like his Maker. Like God
did God make man; man and maid did he make
them.

Genesis 1:26-27 TLB

T he first day of creation was a spectacular event in
time. Reflecting back through Scripture, we can see
the progression of creation. Before God made man,
He completely furnished the earth, just as we furnish our
homes (Genesis 1:1-25). Everything God created reflected
the excellence of its Creator. And it was all designed for the
pinnacle of His creation: Man.

The First Adam

It is interesting to note that God consistently gave the same instructions to every living thing: Each was to reproduce after its own kind, with an emphasis on the word "own." God Himself established the pattern. Now He would create after His own kind a God-kind of being called man. Thus, Adam was a God-man.

> **So God created man in His own image; in the image of God He created him; male and female He created them.**
>
> **Then God blessed them, and God said to them, "Be fruitful and multiply; fill the earth and subdue it; have dominion over the fish of the sea, over the birds of the air, and over every living thing that moves on the earth."**
>
> **Genesis 1:27-28 NKJV**

This is an awesome thought when you consider the implications. Adam, being the first created son of God, was made just like God. This means Adam was like God in nature, like God in ability—at least in regard to the human responsibilities God gave him—and like God in the composition of his being: spirit, soul, and body.

God also made man in His image. In other words, Adam was the exact reflection of God. Adam looked like

God; he talked like God; he thought like God; and he walked like God. Man within his earthly, human context was to function as the god of this world, just as God functions within the context of His eternal deity.

God was not completely satisfied with the depth of fellowship possible with all He previously created, for when He made man, God filled a void that had existed until that moment. Man was the only created being with whom God walked and talked. The angels were like God only in the sense that they were also spirit in nature.

Since Jesus was the Lamb slain before the foundation of the world (Revelation 13:8 NKJB), God must have been making preparations for man for a long time. During the first six days of creation, God set the stage to create His crowning achievement: Man. God meticulously placed everything in position to accommodate this unique God-kind of being—man—who would be so much like God (although he *wasn't* God) that God would be able to fellowship with him on His level.

Think of the powerful significance of that divine plan. It was so thoroughly thought out, so perfectly orchestrated by the mind of God. Every aspect of the plan was precisely as God desired it.

Jesus Christ, the Last Adam

With all this in mind, we can now move ahead in time to Jesus's day:

> **And so it is written, "The first man Adam became a living being." The last Adam became a life-giving spirit.**
>
> **1 Corinthians 15:45** NKJV

Jesus was the replacement of the first Adam:

> **For since by man came death, by Man also came the resurrection of the dead.**
> **For as in Adam all die, even so in Christ all shall be made alive.**
>
> **1 Corinthians 15:21-22** NKJV

The first man Adam corrupted all of creation through sin; the last Adam came to reconcile mankind. Where Adam failed, Jesus was victorious.

Adam, a Son of God—Jesus, God the Son

Adam was the divine expression or likeness of God in the earth. Remember, he was created in the image of God.

Hebrews 1:3 NKJV tells us that when Jesus came, He was also the divine expression of God in the flesh:

> **Who being the brightness of His glory and the express image of His person, and upholding all things by the word of His power, when He had by Himself purged our sins, sat down at the right hand of the Majesty on high.**

The Living Bible helps us see that Jesus was not only an expression of God like His predecessor Adam, but that Jesus also *is* God. We must never lose our point of reference: Adam was a son of God; Jesus is God the Son.

> **God's Son shines out with God's glory, and all that God's Son is and does marks him as God. He regulates the universe by the mighty power of his command. He is the one who died to cleanse us and clear our record of all sin, and then sat down in highest honor beside the great God of heaven.**
> **Hebrews 1:3**

At the same time, let us never forget that the single most selfless substitutionary work in the history of man was when Jesus became a man.

Jesus identified with man so that, ultimately, man could again identify with God. Jesus was man's stand-in.

All that we lost and could not regain as a result of Adam's sin, Jesus—our Lord, our Defender of truth—came to restore. Jesus rescued man from hopelessness and despair, restoring to us eternal life and peace.

In Philippians 2:5-7 RSV, the apostle Paul tells us how this was possible:

Have this mind among yourselves, which is yours in Christ Jesus, who, though he was in the form of God, did not count equality with God a thing to be grasped, but emptied himself, taking the form of a servant, being born in the likeness of men.

Jesus laid aside the privileges of His divinity in order to be born as a man and fulfill God's plan. This did not prevent Him from being God; it simply limited Him in the advantage of *acting* as God. Jesus chose to walk on the earth as a Man. He did all of this for us, ultimately giving His life as a sacrifice to free us from the slavery of sin.

Even at a young age, Jesus understood His destiny. By age twelve, He knew that He had come from God and that God was His Father. Luke 2:52 says that Jesus grew in wisdom and in favor with God and with man. Meanwhile, Jesus continued to develop His security in God as the Son of Man. It was, in fact, His identification with God that astounded the Pharisees.

Jesus's continual reference to God as His Father was the single most aggravating issue that the Pharisees encountered in their clashes with Him. In John 10:30, Jesus actually said, "**I and my Father are one.**" Verse 31 relates the Jews' response to His words: **Then the Jews took up stones again to stone him.** It was this desire of the Jews to destroy the Man who claimed equality with God that eventually brought Jesus to the cross.

I love how Jesus introduced the Father as loving and touchable. Jesus demonstrated in His own life that an intimate relationship with the Father was to be the norm for every believer.

Jesus also revealed that when we are born again, we do not merely receive eternal life or just a spiritual ticket to get into heaven. When we receive eternal life into our spirits, we become members of a holy family with God as our Father. This was God's entire purpose for the creation of the world. He has never lost sight of His original plan or of His ultimate purpose, which is to be united in relationship and in fellowship with man.

'LIKENED UNTO GOD' ON THIS EARTH

Jesus was not crucified either by the common people He helped or by the world. He was crucified by the religious leaders who could not stand to see Him live intimately with the Father and to walk in dominion over this world and its influence.

Religion loses its point of reference and ceases to be pure when it becomes entangled in the opinions of man. As a result, religion fights against the very will and heart of God.

Religion always seems to begin in the mind of man; then it attempts to usurp authority over the mind of God. Religion never allows man to excel in God, for it has the same tendencies as a boa constrictor: it squeezes the life out of a person while staring him in the face. Religious practice apart from the illumination of godly wisdom and truth is deadly.

The religious are still among us today. We dare not speak too often about the worth of redemption or draw too close to the full truth concerning our liberty. When we do, we run the risk of enduring heated opposition from religious people who prefer to erect barriers of man-made reason that prevent people from appropriating the power of God instead of bumping into it by accident.

When we believe what the Bible says—that we are to walk like God in the context of this world—some Christians say we have gone a little too far. And when we declare that we can indeed determine our own destiny in God, we have definitely "pushed the envelope" in the eyes of many believers.

Do we really dare to think of ourselves as equal with God? Certainly we do not consider ourselves equal with Him in the overall sense of His omniscience, omnipresence, or omnipotence. Yet in the context of the specific tasks and assignments God has ordained for us to fulfill both individually and corporately as the body of Christ, in that context we *are* equal with Him. That is the very essence of God's extraordinary plan for man.

In other words, we are authorized, anointed, equipped, commissioned, and commanded to function in the earth as if God were here doing the job for us. Why? Because He is by His Spirit *within* us, doing the job *through* us.

Permit me to develop this thought further through the dialogue between Jesus and the Pharisees found in John 10:30-38 TLB:

> **"I and the Father are one."**
>
> **Then again the Jewish leaders picked up stones to kill him.**
>
> **Jesus said, "At God's direction I have done many a miracle to help the people. For which one are you killing me?"**
>
> **They replied, "Not for any good work, but for blasphemy; you, a mere man, have declared yourself to be God."**
>
> **"In your own Law it says that men are gods!" he replied. "So if the Scripture, which cannot be**

untrue, speaks of those as gods to whom the message of God came, do you call it blasphemy when the one sanctified and sent into the world by the Father says, 'I am the Son of God'?

Don't believe me unless I do miracles of God.

But if I do, believe them even if you don't believe me. Then you will become convinced that the Father is in me, and I in the Father."

To support His claim that He and the Father are one, Jesus quickly turned to the miracles or works He had performed.

The Jews responded to Jesus by stating His so-called "crime," not by glorifying God for His marvelous works. They were not concerned about the miraculous; they were condemning Jesus for what they considered to be blasphemy. They could not handle the fact that this man called Jesus claimed to be one with God and called God His Father.

We, on the other hand, look at this scenario and have no difficulty accepting Jesus referring to Himself as God. However, listen to what Jesus said in verse 34 NKJV in response to their indignation at His claim:

Jesus answered them, "Is it not written in your law, 'I said, "You are gods"'?"

Shouldn't there be a good explanation for what Jesus

was saying? I am also sure that the original language will clear up things and reveal that Jesus was saying exactly what the Father wanted said and understood.

In this passage the Greek word translated "god" is the same as the one for "God." Let's examine the difference between the two:

1. A god or goddess; a general name of deities or divinities

2. The Godhead; the Trinity
    a. God the Father, the first Person in the Trinity
    b. Christ, the second Person in the Trinity
    c. Holy Spirit, the third Person in the Trinity

3. Spoken of the only and true God
    a. Refers to the things of God
    b. His counsels, interests, things due to Him

4. Whatever can in any respect be likened unto God, or resemble Him in any way; God's representative or vice-regent; of magistrates and judges[8]

The only possible interpretation of Jesus's use of the word "god" here is definition number 4. Jesus was saying that we are "likened unto God" and that we "resemble Him in any way."

Notice that the word "representative" is used in this definition. This seems to bring new light to that word. The representatives of the early church acted just like Jesus; they talked just like Him and manifested the power of God just as He did. The people marveled because they knew that the disciples were simple people, yet they could tell by their boldness and authority that they had been with Jesus.

The disciples were acting as an exact representation of Jesus. It was as if Jesus had not left the earth at all. We could even say that it looked as though there were many exact replicas or "clones" of Jesus on the earth.

With this multiplied representation of Jesus on the earth, it is easy to understand why the devil must have been shaking his head, saying, "What was I thinking? I should never have crucified the Lord of glory."

OUR DIVINE COMMISSION

We as the body of Christ are commissioned to do the works of Jesus, as we see in Mark 16:15-20 NKJV:

And He said to them, "Go into all the world and preach the gospel to every creature.

"He who believes and is baptized will be saved; but he who does not believe will be condemned.

"And these signs will follow those who believe: In My name they will cast out demons; they will speak with new tongues;

"They will take up serpents; and if they drink anything deadly, it will by no means hurt them; they will lay hands on the sick, and they will recover."

So then, after the Lord had spoken to them, He was received up into heaven, and sat down at the right hand of God.

And they went out and preached everywhere, the Lord working with them and confirming the word through the accompanying signs. Amen.

The word "commissioned" in the *Webster's Dictionary* means a "formal order granting the power to perform various acts or duties. It is an authorization or command to act in a prescribed manner or to perform prescribed acts."[9]

So if we are likened unto God on the earth and we resemble Him in any way, is it possible that we can do the work of God we have been authorized or commissioned to do just as He would do it? Or more precisely, can we do the work exactly as Jesus did it? Jesus Himself answered that question in John 14:12 when He said that the works I do, you shall do also.

To be sent out to fulfill a commission is to be, in one sense, an "ambassador," meaning "an authorized representative or messenger."[10] The position of ambassador is carried out with the heart and message of the one represented, and it is fortified with the power and might to accomplish the work.

In 2 Corinthians 5:20, we read that God through Jesus has commissioned or sent us on an assignment to take a message to the world.

Now then we are ambassadors for Christ, as though God did beseech you by us: we pray you in Christ's stead, be ye reconciled to God.

In essence, God commissions us in this scripture to go to others and urge them to be reconciled to God. God is responsible for providing whatever it takes to get His message to those to whom He sends it. There is absolutely nothing for us to worry about. If God sends us anywhere as His ambassadors, He pays for our trip and backs us up completely with the evidence and the equipment to support and defend His message.

OUR SPIRITUAL AUTHORITY

Part of the spiritual equipment He provides is the authority to speak in His name and to act on His behalf.

The word "authority" is a legal term, meaning to be invested with rights and power to act on behalf of another. The Greek word is *exousia,* which is defined as "the power of authority (influence) and of right (privilege); the power of rule or government (the power of him whose will and commands must be submitted to by others and obeyed)."[11]

How much divine authority lies at our disposal as believers? Consider the final words of Jesus before He ascended into heaven. Fresh from the greatest battle of all times, from which He emerged the undisputed Victor after rising triumphantly from the grave, Jesus declared, **"All authority in heaven and on earth has been given to me"** (Matthew 28:18 NIV).

Notice, Jesus said *all* authority in heaven and on earth has been given unto Him. Now that same authority has been delegated to us in the name of Jesus to carry out God's will on the earth.

Given this truth, will we allow ourselves to see the definition of the word "authority" in relationship to Jesus's statement, "You are gods"? If indeed what Jesus said carries the validity of the truth—and it most certainly does—then we must take our place, for God has entrusted us with tremendous responsibility. We are to walk in complete dominion over the devil and his works, just as Jesus did when He walked upon the earth.

The question should be asked, "Could the subject of our authority as the sons of God be so vast that we are only scratching the surface of this truth?"

Indeed, the very reason Jesus came to this earth was to demonstrate how we are to walk as the sons of God in this life, having our humanity indwelt by His deity—the Spirit of God residing within the spirit of man.

Only God knows the fullness of the truth that must be comprehended in these last days. Enough of the message must be applied to effectively reach the harvest in time. God needs an army of believers who will go forth boldly and accomplish the mission He has given them. I pray that this book will stimulate you, acting as the "adrenaline" needed to compel you to action, to take your place as a part of that spiritual army.

MAN'S CREATIVE ABILITY TO PRODUCE

When all things are said and done, we will be privileged to comprehend the full significance of what Jesus accomplished for us in this earth and what it means to us on the other side. But for now, I encourage you to look closely once again to the words Jesus spoke in John 10:34 NKJV: **"Is it not written in your law, 'I said, "You are gods"'?"** Then ask yourself this question: "Of whom and to whom is He saying this?"

We have uncovered sufficient evidence as believers to feel somewhat comfortable with these words. But what about the fact that Jesus was talking to unregenerate men when He said this? These men were not born again. In fact, in other passages Jesus called them hypocrites and children of their father the devil. How can this be? Maybe we can tolerate Jesus's calling believers "gods," but how do we explain the fact that He called the unsaved "gods"?

We must understand that God has never stopped viewing man in light of His original plan. God made man in His image and likeness. Even the unregenerate are still in the mold of God. They are spirit (although, of course, they are not partakers of God's nature); they have a soul; and they live in a body. They are on a different road going the wrong way, but they still have the capacity of manifesting the power of their being. What they believe in and act on, they can create.

In this sense, man can be compared to a bread-making machine. We have to put the necessary ingredients into the breadmaker in order to create the desired product. The end result can also be altered according to the ingredients used.

So it is with every one of us. We are so much like God that whatever we think about and meditate on influences our actions. The mechanism of our spirit and soul is designed to function that way. However, what we produce is based on the type of ingredients we allow into our lives.

Once the ingredients are in the bread-making machine, we simply turn it on, and the action of the mechanisms that knead the dough and provide warmth will amazingly produce the bread.

Similarly, once we are convinced by what we accept as truth, we then begin to act on what we believe. Eventually, we produce the results of those core beliefs because it is our divinely designed nature to do so. First Timothy 5:24-25 NKJV is a good reference for this principle of man's creative ability to produce results, whether good or bad:

Some men's sins are clearly evident, preceding them to judgment, but those of some men follow later.

Likewise, the good works of some are clearly evident, and those that are otherwise cannot be hidden.

Mark 11:23 NKJV also refers to the creative nature of man:

"For assuredly, I say to you, whoever says to this mountain, 'Be removed and be cast into the sea,' and does not doubt in his heart, but believes that those things he says will be done, he will have whatever he says."

Psalm 8:4,5 NKJV confirms that God made man creative in nature, just a little lower than Himself:

What is man that You are mindful of him, and the son of man that You visit him?
For You have made him a little lower than the angels, and You have crowned him with glory and honor.

The English word "angels" is a translation of the Hebrew word *Elohim*, meaning "God, god-like, rulers, judges, angels, or gods."[12] All mankind is included in this exalted position, meaning that even fallen man is still above the angelic beings in rank.

Sinful man has lost his heavenly estate; his nature is eternally lost without the redemptive work of Christ. However, he was created with a will and the ability to exercise that will in the earth. If God cannot make everyone accept His provision of salvation, even though it is His ultimate will for us to do so, we can be certain that the devil cannot control man either—*unless* man submits his allegiance to the enemy.

Unfortunately, we often fail to recognize how well the devil has successfully deceived both Christians and non-Christians alike. Yes, the world is cursed, and the devil is the father of those eternally lost. However, God designed man to dominate and master his environment, just as God is the Master of His environment. And the ability to do that was not lost because of the Fall. That ability to act in right standing before God and in accordance with God's divine plan is still available, but only to the born-again portion of the human race.

Tearing Off the Enemy's Blindfold

Second Corinthians 4:3-4 tells us why we need clarification regarding this truth: We need to tear off the enemy's blindfold and begin to build confidence in ourselves so we can become all God created us to be:

> **But if our gospel be hid, it is hid to them that are lost:**
> **In whom the god of this world hath blinded the minds of them which believe not, lest the light of the glorious gospel of Christ, who is the image of God, should shine unto them.**

Notice that the devil is called "the god of this world" in this scripture. Just what is the devil's true position?

The subject of "gods" is more extensive than many have thought. Remember, when God made Adam, He gave him absolute dominion over the works of His hands. Yet today it seems that if anyone is in control, it is the devil. As mentioned earlier, however, man is ranked higher than the devil, so there should be no contest.

So why does the devil seem to dominate this world system with his lies? The temptation of Jesus in Luke 4:5-7 NKJV helps us answer this question.

> **Then the devil, taking Him up on a high mountain, showed Him all the kingdoms of the world in a moment of time.**
>
> **And the devil said to Him, "All this authority I will give You, and their glory; for this has been delivered to me, and I give it to whomever I wish.**
>
> **"Therefore, if You will worship before me, all will be Yours."**

First, the devil said that he had authority over all the earth. If he had been lying, this would not have been a legitimate temptation. Satan said that authority had been delivered to him and that he could give it to whomever he wished.

Where did the devil acquire this authority? We can answer that question based on the enemy's track record: *He stole it,* right? Actually, Adam was the one who had the authority before everything went bad. Before the fall, Adam was too powerful for the devil to steal anything from him. Thus, the situation is clear: When Adam sinned, he delivered to the devil the authority God had given to him.

It was always the devil's intention to usurp authority over God. He could not do it in heaven, so he set out to do it on earth. God did warn Adam of the enemy against whom he would have to guard the garden, one who would attempt to steal everything God had provided for him. This, indeed, was Satan.

It has always been the enemy's plan to use the nature of sin and his authority in the earth to rule over mankind. Yet as we have studied, man has the potential to decide his own fate in many ways. Even fallen man can make decisions that can protect him against some difficulty. Cain, if you will remember, in Genesis 4:7 was instructed by God to rule the sin that was out to destroy him and his brother. Rule is the same word for dominion that God gave Adam and Eve. In the mind of God, Cain had the ability to say no to sin, for that matter, so does the entire human race.

However, because the unbeliever's nature is corrupted by sin, he has no point of reference to make quality decisions. Hatred and selfishness rule his thoughts and desires, causing him to continually act contrary to the will of God. The unbeliever may tame his will and restrain his flesh from indulging in evil ways, but his nature remains set against God.

Given this reality, why shouldn't the Christian rise up in the midst of this lost world with the strength, the character, and the nature of God and move himself and his environment to greatness? Why does it seem so difficult to exercise dominion over the elements of this world? Will there never be an end to the crisis of defeat that so many Christians face?

As long as the devil's deception rules our core beliefs and remains the focus of our awareness, we who are sons and daughters of the Highest will forever submit to the scum of existence, who is Satan.

SUBMITTING TO THE GATHERING OF THE MIGHTY

Now listen to the Lord as He speaks in Psalm 82:1-8:

> **God standeth in the congregation of the mighty; he judgeth among the gods.**
>
> **How long will ye judge unjustly, and accept the persons of the wicked? Selah.**
>
> **Defend the poor and fatherless: do justice to the afflicted and needy.**
>
> **Deliver the poor and needy: rid them out of the hand of the wicked.**
>
> **They know not, neither will they understand; they walk on in darkness: all the foundations of the earth are out of course.**
>
> **I have said, Ye are gods; and all of you are children of the most High.**

> But ye shall die like men, and fall like one of the princes.
>
> Arise, O God, judge the earth: for thou shalt inherit all nations.

This is the passage of Scripture that Jesus was quoting when He said we are all "gods." The first verse says that God (or *Elohim*) stands in the congregation or the gathering of the mighty, which means the ones who are just like God. There He judges among the *Elohim*, which is in plural form.

Notice the injustice of this judging. This would indicate that He is talking to the Israelites, not to those in the church who are born again. He seems to be giving counsel on how to judge correctly. Their judgment in verses 4 and 5 has everything to do with justice being given to needy ones. The ones who need defending seem to be unable to change their course unless someone helps them.

It seems that God is talking to the leaders of the children of Israel. Later in verse 6, He specifies that the people who are being cared for are the children of the Most High.

Remember, when Jesus spoke to the Pharisees, He told them, "I said, you are gods." This indicates that God looks at the leaders of His people as "gods"—which in this context means *those responsible for making right decisions.*

In the midst of a chaotic world where we cannot count on anything to follow God's plan without God's intervention, God sets His people in positions of authority to manifest His goodness. Paul saw this truth in Romans 13:1-6 as God called those in authority "His ministers." We should never take lightly God's structure of given positions and its authority. In verse 6 of Psalm 82, He reiterates the main point of the psalm: **"I have said, Ye are gods."**

Why would God speak this twice, unless it is the primary emphasis of His thought? It is also possible that those who are being spoken to need reinforcement along these lines for encouragement.

Without words being spoken from the "gods," there will be no deliverance. In fact, just the opposite will take place; all will die like mere men. In other words, without divine assistance provided through others to deliver and protect, every human being is doomed.

BELIEVE ME, OR BELIEVE MY WORKS

Let's consider again the account where Jesus confronted the Pharisees' accusations. For the second time, He referred to His works as substantial grounds for proving His claims to be the Son of God. This time He even went out on a limb, as we see in John 10:37-38 NKJV:

"If I do not do the works of My Father, do not believe Me;

**"but if I do, though you do not believe Me,
believe the works, that you may know and believe
that the Father is in Me, and I in Him."**

Jesus was willing to accept the challenge to His authenticity as the Son of God by basing it on whether or not He did the works of God. Do you hear the strength of His conviction?

How many today are willing to say, "If I do not perform the works of God, then don't believe me"?

Jesus went on to say, "And if I do the works of God, even though you choose not to believe the words I speak, you will still be left with the works of God I have completed. At that point you will have to admit that the Father is in Me, and I am in Him."

I know I am being redundant, but I stress this point because Jesus's relationship with the Father and His position in the Father were so real. Likewise, our union with Jesus makes us one with the Father and Jesus in the same measure and same degree that Jesus was and is one with the Father. Even though Jesus's words might be challenged, His works will forever prevail to defend the truth.

Isn't this essentially what Jesus said to us before He ascended to heaven? He said, "Preach the gospel, and the Word you preach will be accompanied with signs and wonders following."

This eternal principle is very simple. Why then are not

many results being produced in the body of Christ? This answer is also very simple: (1) Not many believers are actually believing what God says in His Word, and (2) The Word preached, which we call the gospel, is being watered down with tradition and religion.

The bold preaching of the unfettered Word *will* produce results. Ask the disciples—they relied on this truth to stay alive.

YOU ARE THE PROPHET, KING, AND PRIEST OF YOUR LIFE

Since we are not backed into a corner where results have to be produced, we think it is all right to accommodate our own lack of security by preaching something that produces very little or no results at all.

Individually, we have the responsibility to govern our lives and to rule over circumstances as God would do if He were in our shoes. (By the way, God *is* in our shoes!) Corporately as the body of Christ (and this especially applies to Christian leadership), we have a responsibility to enforce the victory of the Lord Jesus Christ and to demonstrate to the church and to the world the marvelous power of God.

How do we apply all that has been written thus far? With a strong determination to execute our rights and privileges in the earth. Then we can look forward to a life of reigning with Christ:

> **For if by the one man's offense death reigned through the one, much more those who receive abundance of grace and of the gift of righteousness will reign in life through the One, Jesus Christ.**
>
> **Romans 5:17 NKJV**

> **And from Jesus Christ, the faithful witness, the firstborn from the dead, and the ruler over the kings of the earth. To Him who loved us and washed us from our sins in His own blood,**
>
> **and has made us kings and priests to His God and Father, to Him be glory and dominion forever and ever. Amen.**
>
> **Revelation 1:5-6 NKJV**

In the Old Testament, the anointed ones were the prophets, priests, and kings. God put His mantle on these positions to ensure the deliverance and stability of a nation. Jesus fulfilled all these positions while He walked on this earth, and He continues to fulfill them as Savior and Lord over all.

Since our position in Christ is complete (Colossians

2:9,10), and we have received all of His fullness (John 1:16), then these Old Testament positions have now become *our* responsibility.

As the prophets of our own lives, we speak the words of the Holy Ghost, who shows us things to come. The words that God gives us to speak will shape and mold our future for the ultimate glory of God.

As kings, we sit on the throne of our existence. Whether or not we submit to the King of kings for every word spoken and every action taken will determine the force our kingdom will be on the earth. Our words will be obeyed and the kingdom of God will be enhanced and advanced as we release the power and nature of God within us and thus cause the kingdom of Satan to fail.

Finally, as priests we have the responsibility to fulfill our priestly duties. The priest is responsible for holding fast to the command of God and for offering continual sacrifices that are pleasing to God. Let us therefore continually offer up a sacrifice of praise to God, the fruit of our lips, giving thanks in His name (Hebrews 13:15).

I know that the application of these truths to our lives could bring concern to others, since some people might question our humility. And it is true that Paul warned us not to consider ourselves more highly than we ought (Romans 12:3). However, Paul was speaking in relation to other people. We are all in the same class, regardless of our race, ethnic origin, or social level. We are all God's children.

Jesus did humble Himself by accepting and believing in the reality of Who He was. He became a servant to men—the very thing God desires for each one of us. Accepting what God has created us to be and to do will honor Him. Hiding behind some pious doctrine will only serve to elevate our opinion above the omniscience of God.

The most honorable way to walk in the greatness of God's plan is to love one another and be servants to all. But if we don't take the position and the seat of authority God has called us to fill, our love and servanthood will be empty and we will be unable to meet the needs of people.

Jesus Himself said, "You are gods." Let us then begin to act like who and what we are!

Chapter 11

GOD TRAINED MOSES, JESUS TRAINED PAUL, AND PAUL TRAINED TIMOTHY

I realize this chapter has an unusual title, but if you think about it, it pinpoints exactly where the body of Christ is—in training. However, you are greatly mistaken if you think "in training" means that Christians are helpless.

Think about it—hasn't God already done something supernatural to equip and anoint us with His power? If so, why aren't we already going to the harvest fields?

GOD IS LIMITED ONLY BY OUR LACK OF DOING

It seems to be a law of God that as we are busy with what He has given us to do, He continues to make us responsible for more. But if we stay at the gate, always waiting for God to do something, we are essentially blaming God for our own feelings of inadequacy. And in our minds, we begin to make what is not happening in our lives *God's* fault.

This is a serious matter. God is waiting for us to step out in faith. Yes, prayer and being filled with the Holy Spirit are vital parts of any spiritual movement, but the decision to do the works of Jesus is just as vital.

Even as a young boy, I repeatedly witnessed to all my friends about Jesus. Leading people in the sinner's prayer was a common occurrence for me. I didn't know anything about the baptism of the Holy Ghost or the blessing called divine healing; I had no knowledge of gifts of the Spirit. Yet I was persistent enough to act fearlessly on what I did know.

THE TRAINING OF MOSES

The thoughts thus far presented in this chapter are part of the training Moses received. Moses, as we know, was called of the Lord. Already we can see similarities in Moses's life to our lives, for each of us has a call to the ministry of reconciliation. The Great Commission is a divine mandate that authorizes every believer to evangelize the world.

However, the call of God on Moses's life began with a very unique experience.

> Now Moses was tending the flock of Jethro his father-in-law, the priest of Midian. And he led the flock to the back of the desert, and came to Horeb, the mountain of God.
>
> And the Angel of the LORD appeared to him in a flame of fire from the midst of a bush. So he looked, and behold, the bush burned with fire, but the bush was not consumed.
>
> Then Moses said, "I will now turn aside and see this great sight, why the bush does not burn."
>
> So when the LORD saw that he turned aside to look, God called to him from the midst of the bush and said, "Moses, Moses!" And he said, "Here I am."
>
> Then He said, "Do not draw near this place. Take your sandals off your feet, for the place where you stand is holy ground."
>
> **Exodus 3:1-5** NKJV

While Moses was tending sheep near Mount Horeb, the angel of the Lord appeared to him in a flame of fire in the midst of a bush. Moses drew near to get a better look at the curious sight, and when he did, God spoke.

When God sees that we have turned aside from the familiar things of life in order to turn toward Him, He will speak to us just as He did to Moses.

Notice that when Moses was called, he stepped into a holy place. This speaks of the high calling we have as Christians. We are called into a place in the Spirit where we are holy, sanctified, and set apart unto God.

You Are a Deliverer!

As God continued to speak with Moses, He identified Himself as the covenant-keeping God of Abraham, Isaac, and Jacob. Then God began to reveal His intentions. He had seen the oppression of His people, the Israelites. In Exodus 3:8 NKJV, He told Moses, **"So I have come down to deliver them out of the hand of the Egyptians, and to bring them up from that land to a good and large land, to a land flowing with milk and honey."**

If I had been Moses, I might have said, "That's wonderful, Lord—go right ahead and do it." In other words, I might think, "Why are You talking to me, God? If You want the children of Israel delivered so badly, then why don't You just do it?"

The reason God did not deliver the Israelites Himself

is that He must work through man to have entrance into the world. Thank God, He *can* work through us.

An important thought that must be emphasized here is that God called Moses to be a deliverer of His people, which is what Jesus came to do for all the world. That very same call is on our lives. We are to continue the work that Jesus started.

> **"Come now, therefore, and I will send you to Pharaoh that you may bring My people, the children of Israel, out of Egypt."**
>
> **Exodus 3:10 NKJV**

Moses wasn't too excited about this assignment. The first thing he questioned was his qualifications.

Our human nature will always yield to what it knows best. Whenever we lean on our natural reasoning, we will view our assignment according to whether or not we think we have the ability to complete it.

AWARENESS OF GOD'S PRESENCE PRODUCES POWER

If only we would become so heavenly minded and so God conscious that we automatically consider every new assignment and challenge as another opportunity to prove God and His faithfulness!

> But Moses said to God, "Who am I that I should go to Pharaoh, and that I should bring the children of Israel out of Egypt?"
>
> So He said, "I will certainly be with you. And this shall be a sign to you that I have sent you: When you have brought the people out of Egypt, you shall serve God on this mountain."
>
> Exodus 3:11-12 NKJV

God's cure for our inability to produce results is and always has been His presence. When we search the Scriptures for the phrase, "I will be with you," we find that those who believed such were workers of miracles.

At this point, it is easy to tell that Moses was feeling a little better about the potential of this assignment. When Moses asked God for His name, it was evidence that he had accepted what God had commanded him to do:

> Then Moses said to God, "Indeed, when I come to the children of Israel and say to them, 'The God of your fathers has sent me to you,' and they say to me, 'What is His name?' what shall I say to them?"
>
> And God said to Moses, "I AM WHO I AM." And He said, "Thus you shall say to the children of Israel, 'I AM has sent me to you.'"
>
> Exodus 3:13-14 NKJV

Do you remember what Peter said to the man at the gate of the temple who was impotent in his feet? With boldness, the apostle declared: **Such as I have give I thee: In the name of Jesus Christ of Nazareth rise up and walk** (Acts 3:6).

By using the authority in the name of Jesus, Peter was acting in Jesus's stead. In the same way, God was giving Moses the authority to act in His stead. God then proceeded to reveal His plan to Moses for delivering the children of Israel.

SHOW AND TELL

In Exodus, chapter 4, Moses questioned what to do if the people didn't listen to him. I think it is interesting that God had everything figured out, just as He does when He gives us *our* assignments.

In verse 2 NKJV, God asked Moses, **"What is that in your hand?"**

"A rod," Moses replied.

God then proceeded to show Moses two miracles that Moses could use as proof of God's presence and His ability to supernaturally deliver His people. Through these supernatural demonstrations, Moses immediately learned the value of signs and wonders.

If signs and wonders were a part of God's plan then,

they are certainly a part of His plan today. Jesus confirmed this in John 4:48 NKJV: **Then Jesus said to him, "Unless you people see signs and wonders, you will by no means believe."**

If you look up this verse in the original language, you will find that Jesus was essentially saying, "Unless you people see signs and wonders, you cannot and will not believe."

God understands the will and the heart of man. He knows we must demonstrate what we speak. God did not originate the game hide-and-seek. If He had, we never would have found Him. (See Jeremiah 29:13.) However, He did originate the show-and-tell activity so we could see and believe. Then He gave us the job of showing and telling others so they too could come to see, hear, and believe.

But whether we show people and then tell them or tell them and then show them, the connection between demonstration and the spoken Word is by divine design. It is all a part of God's plan for capturing the attention and conscience of man. Man's heart must be turned *from* this world *toward* Him, and God seems to indicate that it will take both precept *and* example to accomplish this goal.

It is common knowledge that a person will only comprehend a small amount of what is told to him. If someone both tells him *and* shows him, that person will receive a much greater understanding of the subject under discussion. But he will receive the greatest depth of understanding when someone *tells* him, *shows* him, and then *invites him to participate.*

Throughout Exodus 4, God continued to convince Moses of His supernatural ability that would accompany him. Even though God was convincing, Moses still felt inadequate and asked God to allow someone else to do the job. God comforted Moses by allowing his brother Aaron to assist him.

KNOW YOUR POSITION

In Exodus 4:15-16 NKJV, God spoke to Moses concerning the chain of command between him and Aaron and the perspective through which Moses should see his position:

> **"Now you shall speak to him and put the words in his mouth. And I will be with your mouth and with his mouth, and I will teach you what you shall do.**
>
> **"So he shall be your spokesman to the people. And he himself shall be as a mouth for you, and you shall be to him as God."**

Catch the importance of what God was saying to Moses: "Aaron shall be as you to My people, speaking the

words that I give you, and you shall be as God to him."
God wanted Moses to become one with His thoughts. In
Exodus 7:1, God reiterated the importance of Moses's
position as a deliverer by saying "See, I have made you as
God to Pharoah." God was encouraging Moses to see
the potential of this God-given assignment. Whether or
not Moses could see it would be the determining factor in
the end results.

This is all a part of Moses's training. Moses must
develop his conscience to see and accept the responsibility
of being made by God as God to Pharaoh.

Then in verse 17, God revealed to Moses the signet of
His presence—the rod in Moses's hand. God's words in
the mouth of Moses, and the presence of God in his hand,
would deliver the children of Israel from the Egyptians.

What a wonderful combination!

Today things have only changed for the better. Not
only can we still put God's Word in our mouth and hold
God's power in our hands, but He has also come to abide
and dwell in our hearts.

Moses proved faithful in the small things as he led the
children of Israel out of Egypt. Yet God would test him to
see how much he had learned about his position.

In Exodus 14, when the children of Israel came to the
Red Sea, God would hold Moses responsible for their
deliverance. With mountains looming above them on each
side, the sea stretched out before them, and Pharaoh's

army closing in behind them, the people of God needed a miracle:

> And Moses said to the people, "Do not be afraid. Stand still, and see the salvation of the LORD, which He will accomplish for you today. For the Egyptians whom you see today, you shall see again no more forever.
>
> "The LORD will fight for you, and you shall hold your peace."
>
> And the LORD said to Moses, "Why do you cry to Me? Tell the children of Israel to go forward.
>
> "But lift up your rod, and stretch out your hand over the sea and divide it. And the children of Israel shall go on dry ground through the midst of the sea."
>
> Exodus 14:13-16 NKJV

Consider the way that The Living Bible paraphrases this passage:

> But Moses told the people, "Don't be afraid. Just stand where you are and watch, and you will see the wonderful way the Lord will rescue you today. The Egyptians you are looking at—you will never see them again.

"The Lord will fight for you, and you won't need to lift a finger!"

Then the Lord said to Moses, "Quit praying and get the people moving! Forward, march!

Use your rod—hold it out over the water, and the sea will open up a path before you, and all the people of Israel shall walk through on dry ground!"

QUIT PRAYING AND GET MOVING

Notice how wonderful the words of Moses sound in verses 13 and 14 of Exodus 14. The words are definitely bold about what God would do and what the children of Israel should expect. There was only one small problem. Moses was waiting for God to do something. He was forgetting the equation that God had given him.

Moses had forgotten that he was in the position of God and that the rod he held in his hand was the presence of God to perform the work. As Moses did his part, so God would do His part.

Let's look again at the way The Living Bible records God's instructions to Moses in this situation: **"Quit praying and get the people moving! Forward, march! Use your rod—hold it out over the water"** (vv. 15-16). Can you see that God rebuked Moses for not assuming the position He had delegated to him? Before that divine rebuke, Moses considered the problem bigger than the ability of God that had already been given to him.

How easy it is for us to jump right in the middle of Moses's mentality as he stood between Pharaoh's army and the Red Sea. Consider this:

- Do you sometimes beg God to do something to get you out of the seemingly impossible situation you are facing?
- When you tell everyone around you what God is going to do for you, are you really hinting to God that He needs to do something quickly?
- Are you praying when you should be acting?
- If you haven't received an answer to your prayer, could it be that you already know what to do, but you're trying to get God to tell you again?

If you answered yes to any of these questions, can you guess what is necessary for you to overcome in the situation you're facing? Probably the same thing that was necessary in Moses's situation: *action!*

We can certainly learn much from Moses's training. The very question that Moses started with—"Who am I?"—was the evidence that he had further training to complete with God.

THE TRAINING OF PAUL

From earlier studies, we know that Jesus was successful because He knew who He was. As we consider the Pauline revelation, we can see that it primarily focuses on how the redemptive work of the Lord Jesus Christ—His death, burial, resurrection, and ascension—affects the Christian. The believer, then, becomes successful in his spiritual walk as he learns who he is in Christ. With all this in mind, let's look briefly at how Jesus trained the apostle Paul.

Paul had a tremendous conversion experience on the road to Damascus:

> **Then Saul, still breathing threats and murder against the disciples of the Lord, went to the high priest**
>
> **And asked letters from him to the synagogues of Damascus, so that if he found any who were of the Way, whether men or women, he might bring them bound to Jerusalem.**
>
> **And as he journeyed he came near Damascus, and suddenly a light shone around him from heaven.**
>
> **Then he fell to the ground, and heard a voice saying to him, "Saul, Saul, why are you persecuting Me?"**

And he said, "Who are You, Lord?" Then the Lord said, "I am Jesus, whom you are persecuting. It is hard for you to kick against the goads."

So he, trembling and astonished, said, "Lord, what do You want me to do?" Then the Lord said to him, "Arise and go into the city, and you will be told what you must do."

Acts 9:1-6 NKJV

As Paul retold his conversion experience in Acts 22:15, he repeated something else that was said to him by Ananias about Jesus, whom Paul had met on the road: **For thou shalt be his witness unto all men of what thou hast seen and heard.**

PAUL'S APPLICATION OF REVELATION

In Paul's experience, he both heard and saw the Lord. In his writings, he revealed that he had many such spiritual experiences, all of which had great significance in his life and ministry:

It is doubtless not profitable for me to boast. I will come to visions and revelations of the Lord:

I know a man in Christ who fourteen years ago—whether in the body I do not know, or

whether out of the body I do not know, God knows—such a one was caught up to the third heaven.

And I know such a man—whether in the body or out of the body I do not know, God knows—

how he was caught up into Paradise and heard inexpressible words, which it is not lawful for a man to utter.

Of such a one I will boast; yet of myself I will not boast, except in my infirmities.

For though I might desire to boast, I will not be a fool; for I will speak the truth. But I refrain, lest anyone should think of me above what he sees me to be or hears from me.

And lest I should be exalted above measure by the abundance of the revelations, a thorn in the flesh was given to me, a messenger of Satan to buffet me, lest I be exalted above measure.

2 Corinthians 12:1-7 NKJV

The full extent of Paul's experiences is recorded in the epistles he wrote. He tells us that there was an abundance of revelations given to him. The devil greatly opposed these revelations lest the truth of the redemption be told and his deception exposed. Throughout these wonderful experiences, the Lord was teaching Paul the mystery of the ages that must be revealed:

> Dear friends, I solemnly swear that the way to heaven which I preach is not based on some mere human whim or dream.
>
> For my message comes from no less a person than Jesus Christ himself, who told me what to say. No one else has taught me.
>
> Galatians 1:11-12 TLB

Very simply put, Jesus trained Paul in the revelation and the application of the message. Jesus's message revealed through the Pauline epistles is so vital because it resurrects the failing heart of the confused and the wearied and again brings victory into an obtainable reach.

Read for a moment what Paul said and did as we follow some of his successes:

> Now when they had passed through Amphipolis and Apollonia, they came to Thessalonica, where there was a synagogue of the Jews.
>
> Then Paul, as his custom was, went in to them, and for three Sabbaths reasoned with them from the Scriptures,
>
> explaining and demonstrating that the Christ had to suffer and rise again from the dead, and saying, "This Jesus whom I preach to you is the Christ."
>
> Acts 17:1-3 NKJV

Here we see Paul preaching and teaching in the synagogues of Thessalonica. In verse 2, notice the phrase that should by now be familiar to our ears: **Then Paul,** *as his custom was,* **went in to them.** Where were the Jews Paul was preaching to? In the synagogue.

THE MESSAGE AND METHODS OF JESUS PRODUCE RESULTS

Where have we heard this before? We need only to think back on the ministry of Jesus.

> **And he came to Nazareth, where he had been brought up: and,** *as his custom was,* **he went into the synagogue on the sabbath day, and stood up for to read.**
>
> **And there was delivered unto him the book of the prophet Esaias. And when he had opened the book, he found the place where it was written,**
>
> **The Spirit of the Lord is upon me, because he hath anointed me to preach the gospel to the poor; he hath sent me to heal the brokenhearted, to preach deliverance to the captives, and recovering of sight to the blind, to set at liberty them that are bruised,**
>
> **To preach the acceptable year of the Lord.**
>
> **Luke 4:16-19**

If Jesus was Paul's teacher—and He was—it shouldn't surprise us that Paul developed the same custom that Jesus practiced. If a person is associated with someone long enough, he begins to pick up on that person's mannerisms.

Paul did more than adopt Jesus's mannerisms; he copied the message Jesus preached. Why did Jesus preach these Scriptures everywhere He went? Because this message produced results.

I believe that Jesus not only revealed to Paul the revelation of redemption, but He also explained to Paul how to produce results. Acts 17:3 NKJV says that Paul both *explained* and *demonstrated* that Jesus was the Christ.

It must have been easy for Paul to explain to people that Jesus is the Christ. Anything seen through hindsight is seen with 20/20 vision.

Paul was a Pharisee of the Pharisees. He had studied all about the Messiah. Therefore, when Paul came to realize that Jesus really *was* the Christ, I'm sure all his earlier studies suddenly became increasingly clear.

So how do we demonstrate that Jesus is the Christ as Paul did? If Jesus is the Christ, or the Anointed One, and He is living in the hearts of all of us who believe, there ought to be evidence of His power in our lives.

This is certainly confirmed by what Jesus said to the disciples before He left this earth: **And, behold, I send the promise of my Father upon you: but tarry ye in the city** of Jerusalem, until ye be endued with power from on high (Luke 24:49).

Then in Acts 1:8-9 NKJV, we read this:

> "But you shall receive power when the Holy Spirit has come upon you; and you shall be witnesses to Me in Jerusalem, and in all Judea and Samaria, and to the end of the earth."
>
> Now when He had spoken these things, while they watched, He was taken up, and a cloud received Him out of their sight.

Jesus told the disciples that they needed to be endued with power by the Holy Spirit in order to be witnesses for Him.

The word "witness" means "those whose lives and actions testify to the worth and effect of faith and whose faith received "witness" in Scripture; First Peter 5:1."[13] The endowment of power through the Holy Ghost is the distinguishing difference that made the lives of the apostles resemble Jesus. The world will recognize that Jesus is alive by the evidence produced.

Notice what the disciples did in obedience to Jesus's instructions:

> And when they had prayed, the place where they were assembled together was shaken; and

they were all filled with the Holy Spirit, and they spoke the word of God with boldness.

Now the multitude of those who believed were of one heart and one soul; neither did anyone say that any of the things he possessed was his own, but they had all things in common.

And with great power the apostles gave witness to the resurrection of the Lord Jesus. And great grace was upon them all.

Acts 4:31-33 NKJV

With great power, the apostles provided evidence of the resurrection of the Lord Jesus. Paul learned that through the power of the message (1 Corinthians 1:17-18) and by the power of the Holy Ghost, he should expect demonstrations to occur.

First Thessalonians 1:5-7 NKJV shows us the results of Paul's method of ministry in which he both explained and demonstrated the Word:

For our gospel did not come to you in word only, but also in power, and in the Holy Spirit and in much assurance, as you know what kind of men we were among you for your sake.

And you became followers of us and of the Lord, having received the word in much affliction, with joy of the Holy Spirit,

so that you became examples to all in
Macedonia and Achaia who believe.

The phrase, **"for our gospel did not come to you in
word only, but also in power"** (v. 5), was a result of Paul's
training under the Lord Jesus Christ Himself. Because
Paul expected the miraculous in his ministry, the miraculous always occurred.

Verse 6 says that the Thessalonian believers became
"followers," or as other translations say, "imitators." They
saw such life in Paul, in his message, and in the results of
his preaching that they desired to be imitators of the same.

Then in verse 7, we see further reason to rejoice. The
Thessalonian Christians also became examples, which can
be translated as *models*. Models of what? Models of the
apostle Paul, who was a model of the Lord Jesus Christ.
Paul reiterated this thought in 1 Corinthians 11:1 NKJV:
Imitate me, just as I also imitate Christ.

We have a lot of imitating to catch up on, don't we?

Every situation with a diversity of new experiences
should cause us to reevaluate our findings in light of the
truth of Christ. No matter what we know, we must become
increasingly proficient in the application of that knowledge.

As we look at Paul's ministry in Athens, we can see
how well he ministered both by precept and example:

Now while Paul waited for them at Athens, his spirit was provoked within him when he saw that the city was given over to idols.

Therefore he reasoned in the synagogue with the Jews and with the Gentile worshipers, and in the marketplace daily with those who happened to be there.

Then certain Epicurean and Stoic philosophers encountered him. And some said, "What does this babbler want to say?" Others said, "He seems to be a proclaimer of foreign gods," because he preached to them Jesus and the resurrection.

And they took him and brought him to the Areopagus, saying, "May we know what this new doctrine is of which you speak?

"For you are bringing some strange things to our ears. Therefore we want to know what these things mean."

For all the Athenians and the foreigners who were there spent their time in nothing else but either to tell or to hear some new thing.

Then Paul stood in the midst of the Areopagus and said, "Men of Athens, I perceive that in all things you are very religious;

"for as I was passing through and considering the objects of your worship, I even found an altar with this inscription: TO THE UNKNOWN

GOD. Therefore, the One whom you worship without knowing, Him I proclaim to you:

"God, who made the world and everything in it, since He is Lord of heaven and earth, does not dwell in temples made with hands.

"Nor is He worshiped with men's hands, as though He needed anything, since He gives to all life, breath, and all things.

"And He has made from one blood every nation of men to dwell on all the face of the earth, and has determined their preappointed times and the boundaries of their dwellings,

"so that they should seek the Lord, in the hope that they might grope for Him and find Him, though He is not far from each one of us;

"for in Him we live and move and have our being, as also some of your own poets have said, 'For we are also His offspring.'

"Therefore, since we are the offspring of God, we ought not to think that the Divine Nature is like gold or silver or stone, something shaped by art and man's devising.

"Truly, these times of ignorance God overlooked, but now commands all men everywhere to repent,

"because He has appointed a day on which He will judge the world in righteousness by the Man whom He has ordained. He has given assurance of this to all by raising Him from the dead."

And when they heard of the resurrection of the dead, some mocked, while others said, "We will hear you again on this matter."

So Paul departed from among them.

However, some men joined him and believed, among them Dionysius the Areopagite, a woman named Damaris, and others with them.

Acts 17:16-34 NKJV

The Purpose of Evidence

Athens was a very philosophical city, steeped in tradition. With all the genius of his mind, Paul tried his best to reason with the Athenians on their level. Yet the greatest response he received is revealed in verse 32: **"We will hear you again on this matter."** A few people believed, but their number was certainly not what Paul had expected. Interesting to note: Athens was the only city in which Paul didn't establish a church and there were no miracles recorded.

Could Paul have done a better job? I really don't know, yet I can see something stirring in him in the next meeting he held. In Acts 18:1, we are told that Paul went next to the city of Corinth. We have record in 1 Corinthians 2:1-5 NKJV of how Paul approached the Corinthians:

And I, brethren, when I came to you, did not come with excellence of speech or of wisdom declaring to you the testimony of God.

For I determined not to know anything among you except Jesus Christ and Him crucified.

I was with you in weakness, in fear, and in much trembling.

And my speech and my preaching were not with persuasive words of human wisdom, but in demonstration of the Spirit and of power,

that your faith should not be in the wisdom of men but in the power of God.

I wonder if the reason Paul came in fear and trembling was that his confidence after Athens was in need of a boost. He purposely went back to the simplicity of preaching Christ—something he was sure would produce results. This platform allowed the Holy Ghost liberty to manifest Himself with demonstrations of power.

Now, we must be careful not to judge a service by whether or not there are demonstrations of power. Sometimes services have certain purposes in which a demonstration of power is not necessary. Many times Jesus talked with the disciples, explaining to them secrets concerning the kingdom of God. During these times, no supernatural demonstrations took place.

We must seek to find God's balance between the different types of services and the specific purpose for each service. However, in this discussion we are focusing on the ministry of Jesus. As He was presented with occasions to bring deliverance to people, consistent manifestations of divine power occurred.

Paul was learning to rely on the same understanding to produce evidence at the appropriate time. He became very productive in his ministry because of how he had been trained. When opposition arose, he became extremely bold in his declaration of the gospel, and demonstrations of God's power were the inevitable result.

THE TRAINING OF TIMOTHY

It was this understanding of how to produce results in ministry that Paul passed on to a young minister named Timothy.

Paul undertook to teach Timothy and to prepare him for his future as a minister of the gospel. In 1 Timothy 1:2, Paul began instructing his young disciple by encouraging him as a true son in the faith. Later in the first chapter, Paul again encouraged him because of those who were blaspheming the faith:

This charge I commit to you, son Timothy, according to the prophecies previously made

concerning you, that by them you may wage the good warfare,

having faith and a good conscience, which some having rejected, concerning the faith have suffered shipwreck,

of whom are Hymenaeus and Alexander, whom I delivered to Satan that they may learn not to blaspheme.

1 Timothy 1:18-20 NKJV

Paul wonderfully encouraged Timothy by reminding the younger man that he possessed faith and a good conscience—necessary qualities for waging a good warfare. Paul continued to weave these thoughts throughout this letter and on into his second letter to Timothy. Paul wanted to make sure Timothy understood that strong faith was necessary to stand his ground and progress in the message of Christ.

In 1 Timothy 3:13 NKJV, Paul wrote, **For those who have served well as deacons obtain for themselves a good standing and great boldness in the faith which is in Christ Jesus.**

In chapter 4, Paul went on to admonish young Timothy with godly counsel that all believers and ministers should heed:

Let no one despise your youth, but be an example to the believers in word, in conduct, in love, in spirit, in faith, in purity.

Till I come, give attention to reading, to exhortation, to doctrine.

Do not neglect the gift that is in you, which was given to you by prophecy with the laying on of the hands of the eldership.

Meditate on these things; give yourself entirely to them, that your progress may be evident to all.

Take heed to yourself and to the doctrine. Continue in them, for in doing this you will save both yourself and those who hear you.

1 Timothy 4:12-16 NKJV

Paul exhorted Timothy to walk in love, to display godly character, and to study with undivided attention. He also warned Timothy not to neglect the gift that was in him. The purpose behind Paul's counsel was to make Timothy's progress evident to all as the young man meditated on and applied these principles to his life. It was Paul's desire that Timothy's life be a living example of the power of the Lord Jesus.

As Paul closed his first letter to Timothy, he again strongly urged Timothy to fight the good fight of faith (1 Timothy 6:12). The best way to fight a good fight is to win. Therefore, everything Paul said can be summed up as encouragement to help Timothy obtain the victory God had already ordained for him.

We can all be encouraged by Paul's words, just as Timothy was no doubt encouraged. We just have to grasp the truth that what we have in Christ is more than enough. Winning in every situation is just a matter of holding fast to the life of God and everything He has done.

STIR UP THE GIFT

In Paul's second letter to Timothy, Paul began again by admonishing him to be a faithful doer of the truth.

Sometimes when we are starting out in ministry, or even if we have been at it awhile, we need encouragement to remain steadfast. Encouraging others along this line seemed to be part of Paul's calling.

Timothy must have been questioning both his ability and his faith, as we can see in the beginning of 2 Timothy 1. Paul started out by immediately reminding him that prayers were going up night and day on his behalf (2 Timothy 1:3).

Then Paul set out to remind Timothy of the truth that had been planted deep in Timothy's spirit. He urged Timothy to remember that the kind of faith he possessed was the unfeigned faith of his grandmother Lois and his mother Eunice (2 Timothy 1:5). Knowing that this deep-rooted faith resided within Timothy, Paul told him, **Stir up the gift of God which is in you** (v. 6 NKJV).

Paul gave a similar exhortation in his first letter (1 Timothy 4:14). Being mindful is the first step to doing something about anything.

When I was growing up, I can remember when Nestles Quik came as a chocolate powder in a can. Then the manufacturer introduced Nestles Quik in syrup form. This was exciting to me as a kid because it was easier to mix and use.

I remember squeezing a bunch of chocolate syrup into a glass of cold milk and watching it sink to the bottom. At that point, the only way I knew that syrup was in there was that I was the one who had poured it in the glass.

I lifted the glass and looked; there was all that syrup at the bottom. Chocolate was in the milk, but it wasn't chocolate milk yet. Only after I put the spoon in the glass and started stirring did the two substances mix together and become chocolate milk.

That's a good way to illustrate Paul's aim in writing these letters to Timothy. Paul wanted his young disciple to start using his faith to stir up the spiritual deposits in his heart. As Timothy did this, he would become more aware of the One Who lived in his heart so he could become more of the man God had created him to be.

When we become aware of the Greater One in us, fear is the first thing to leave. This is what Paul addressed next. In 2 Timothy 1:7 NKJV, he wrote, **For God has not given us a spirit of fear, but of power and of love and of a sound mind.**

The word translated "fear" in this verse could also be translated "timidity." God has not made us timid, but with

His power, His love, and a mind that masters all circumstances, we are strong and courageous.

These words of encouragement, along with the consistent love of the apostle Paul, turned Timothy into a mighty man of God, as we see from Paul's later writings:

> **For a great door and effectual is opened unto me, and there are many adversaries.**
>
> **Now if Timotheus come, see that he may be with you without fear: for he worketh the work of the Lord, as I also do.**
>
> **1 Corinthians 16:9-10**

One thing we know for sure from the Scriptures is the way the apostle Paul conducted business when entering a new work. He preached the simple gospel message and demonstrated it with the Holy Ghost and power. So if Paul were working with an individual who consistently operated in fear, he wouldn't describe the times he ministered with that person as "effectual." Fear greatly hinders the message of the gospel.

Knowing this, I wasn't satisfied with the translation of this passage of Scripture that makes Timothy still seem very susceptible to fear. Later I found that the *Amplified Bible* translation makes better sense. It is the translation that best supports what Paul produced in Timothy, and it best explains why Timothy's help was being sought:

> When Timothy arrives, see to it that [you put him at ease, so that] he may be fearless among you, for he is [devotedly] doing the Lord's work, just as I am. So [see to it that] no one despises him or treats him as if he were of no account or slights him. But send him off [cordially, speed him on his way] in peace, that he may come to me, for I am expecting him [to come along] with the other brethren.
>
> 1 Corinthians 16:10-11

In order to work the works of God, we have to know something about who we are and what we possess. Consider what Jesus said in John 9:4 NKJV in response to His disciples' questions about a man who was born blind and whom He intended to heal: **"I must work the works of Him who sent Me."** As we have already seen, what Jesus did and who Jesus knew Himself to be continually worked together to produce results for God's Kingdom.

Paul desired someone to accompany him into the province of Asia who possessed the knowledge of how to use the equipment of God. Paul knew that conversions would be numerous if the works of God were demonstrated the way Jesus had emphatically promised they would be:

> **"Most assuredly, I say to you, he who believes in Me, the works that I do he will do also; and**

greater works than these he will do, because I go to My Father."

John 14:12 NKJV

This is what Jesus said *would* happen; this is what *must* happen; and this is what *will* happen as we apply these scriptural principles to our lives.

Our part is simple—we just have to allow the Holy Spirit to bring us to His training grounds. There He will teach us the mysteries of who we are in Christ. There we will also learn how to use the spiritual equipment He has already provided so that we can do the greater works we are called to do on His behalf.

Chapter 12

WHEN YOU KNOW, THE POWER FLOWS

**Now faith is the substance of things hoped for,
the evidence of things not seen.**

Hebrews 11:1 NKJV

As you consider doing the works of Jesus, you may honestly feel that you are really not anointed. For that matter, there may be times when you don't even feel very saved. Yes, the Word of God gives many reasons why you *shouldn't* feel inadequate, but the truth may be that you still do.

That's why Hebrews 11:1 is such a comforting verse. In essence it says that your faith is the substance of all the things that are real in God, even when you don't feel like they are real at all.

Faith is the substance of your salvation and of your anointing. It is also the substance of the strength and confidence you need to overcome your inadequacies so you can stop feeling like you're not able when you really are.

We are a blessed people to have faith as our method of operation. With faith, there are no limitations except the ones we place on ourselves when we are not willing to believe what God has already promised us.

DECLARING WHAT IS *NOT YET* AS THOUGH IT ALREADY *IS*

Faith becomes inspired and usable when the will of God is known, for faith needs concrete evidence to exist. The strength of our faith is the strength of God's Word. That means the Word must be perceived as absolute and certain in order for faith to work.

Have you ever noticed in the Word of God that where faith is exercised, it always operates in the *now*, in the present tense? As we discussed earlier, the language of Jesus was much different from that of the Pharisees. He declared things that couldn't be seen initially as though they already were.

Jesus's commands were always filled with faith. For instance, to the man with the withered hand, Jesus said, "Stretch out your hand" (Matthew 12:13 NKJV). Jesus didn't refer to the problem, saying, "Give Me your arm with the withered hand on it." Instead, He declared what the man was to do at that immediate moment to obtain his healing—something that to the man's natural eyes could not be done.

Another example of this principle can be found where Jesus spoke to the disciples about His role as the Shepherd of the sheep. Jesus said to them:

> **"And when he brings out his own sheep, he goes before them; and the sheep follow him, for they know his voice.**
>
> **"Yet they will by no means follow a stranger, but will flee from him, for they do not know the voice of strangers."**
>
> **John 10:4-5** NKJV

Later in this same chapter, Jesus said this:

> **"I am the good shepherd; and I know My sheep, and am known by My own.**
>
> **"As the Father knows Me, even so I know the Father; and I lay down My life for the sheep."**
>
> **John 10:14-15** NKJV

Jesus said that His sheep hear His voice and they know Him. Notice He *didn't* say that they have to work at hearing His voice or that they only believe they know Him.

This latter way requires a lot of effort but not any faith. However, if we take Jesus's words literally, we have to conclude by faith that we all know Him and we can all hear His voice.

Personally, I say this all the time: "Lord, I thank You that I do know You and that I always hear Your voice."

As we speak these words, we are agreeing with what the Lord has said about us. Thus, we have a basis for results as our faith is exercised in the absolute faithfulness of God to perform His Word.

In John 8, Jesus explained this same principle: "**And you shall know the truth, and the truth shall make you free**" (John 8:32 NKJV).

If the truth could make us free all by itself, it would have already done so in all our lives. However, it is the truth we *know* that sets us free.

I grew up knowing from a young age that Jesus died for my sins. As a result, I accepted Him as my Savior. Although I was saved, I did not yet know that salvation includes healing. Therefore, I could not take advantage of that particular truth; it could not set me free from sickness and disease.

We can also see this principle in operation in Matthew 16:13-19 NKJV:

When Jesus came into the region of Caesarea Philippi, He asked His disciples, saying, "Who do men say that I, the Son of Man, am?"

So they said, "Some say John the Baptist, some Elijah, and others Jeremiah or one of the prophets."

He said to them, "But who do you say that I am?"

And Simon Peter answered and said, "You are the Christ, the Son of the living God."

Jesus answered and said to him, "Blessed are you, Simon Bar-Jonah, for flesh and blood has not revealed this to you, but My Father who is in heaven.

"And I also say to you that you are Peter, and on this rock I will build My church, and the gates of Hades shall not prevail against it.

"And I will give you the keys of the kingdom of heaven, and whatever you bind on earth will be bound in heaven, and whatever you loose on earth will be loosed in heaven."

If the fact that Jesus is the Christ could automatically keep the gates of hell from prevailing against the church, it would have already done so. But the truth each person *knows for himself* is the truth that sets him free.

Yes, it is true that Jesus is the Christ. But whether or not we personally know Him as Christ determines how the gates of hell will respond to *us*.

First John 5:14-15 NKJV serves to persuade us even further regarding this principle:

Now this is the confidence that we have in Him, that if we ask anything according to His will, He hears us.

And if we know that He hears us, whatever we ask, we know that we have the petitions that we have asked of Him.

John begins this passage with a powerful message regarding confidence. He is even going to tell us how confidence is defined: **This is the confidence that we have** *in Him.*

True confidence is found in no one else but God. But there is a condition here. Notice the "if" with which John begins the next phrase: *If* **we ask anything** *according to His will...*

The will of God is simply His Word. He didn't write the Bible so He could remember what He believed. He wrote it so we would know His will and His heart's desire for us.

When we pray the will of God, He immediately hears us. This is an automatic consequence of our prayers, as long as we know God's will.

I'll put it another way. If we have a Bible fact or promise about what God has done for us or what we can expect Him to do, all we have to do is pray according to that promise. When we do, God will hear us. This is an absolute truth we can count on; there is no question about it.

The next verse says, **And *if we know that He hears us...*** Does this mean that it is possible to pray the will of God and not know that God has heard? Yes, people do it all the time. They pray and then wait for the answer to show up so they can know that they actually believed when they prayed.

Doesn't it make sense that it is too late to start believing if we have already seen the answer to our prayers? God wants us to use faith *when we pray.*

John continues to build his case: **And if we know that He hears us, whatever we ask, we know that we have the petitions that we have asked of Him** (v. 15).

Jesus gave us the same principle when He said: **He that believeth on the Son hath everlasting life** (John 3:36). In other words, *believing is possessing.*

Why do we see answers to our petitions? Because we know the will of God; we know He hears us when we pray; and we know we have what we have asked for. This is the confidence born of true faith.

Now let's look at 1 John 5:11-13 NKJV:

> **And this is the testimony: that God has given us eternal life, and this life is in His Son.**
>
> **He who has the Son has life; he who does not have the Son of God does not have life.**

These things I have written to you who believe in the name of the Son of God, that you may know that you have eternal life, and that you may continue to believe in the name of the Son of God.

John talks about eternal life and its importance in verses 11 and 12. Then in verse 13, he states the reason he wrote this epistle: so we may know that we have eternal life. According to this passage of Scripture, knowing we have eternal life is the reason it works in our lives.

How many people do you know who possess eternal life, yet that divine life doesn't seem to have any noticeable effect on their lives? They surely know they have eternal life, but they don't know how it works.

The answer is simple. Only as we come to realize what it means to have eternal life does that life begin to flow in and through our lives in a way we can see and experience.

You see, it isn't enough for us to understand that we possess something from God. We must also know that it will begin to work in our lives as soon as we start believing in what we possess.

ELIJAH AND ELISHA: WORKING WITH THE ANOINTING

There are two men we have to talk about who used the anointing with great confidence. These men were Old Testament prophets anointed by the Holy Spirit, and their names were Elijah and Elisha.

Elisha followed Elijah in ministry and, at Elijah's death, received double the anointing that had been upon his master. The amazing thing about both these prophets is that they comprehended so well and understood so completely how to use the anointing God had provided as spiritual equipment for their prophetic ministry. They were so confident about what they possessed that at times when God wasn't initiating anything, they used their own faith and the anointing produced similar results.

In 1 Kings 18:1 NKJV, we read about a time when God sent Elijah with a message for the wicked King Ahab and Queen Jezebel:

> **And it came to pass after many days that the words of the LORD came to Elijah, in the third year, saying, "Go, present yourself to Ahab, and I will send rain on the earth."**

This Elijah did according to the word of the Lord. God initiated this situation, but there was no word of the Lord for the scene that took place next on top of Mount

Carmel. There, Elijah challenged the 450 prophets of Baal and the 400 prophets of Asherah to a contest (1 Kings 18:17-40).

The basis for Elijah's challenge was the commandment of God: **Thou shalt have no other gods before me** (Exodus 20:3). Elijah had the written Word as the general basis for his challenge, but he had no specific word of the Lord for it. Nevertheless, Elijah's faith to challenge this sin with the anointing brought the fire of God down to consume the sacrifice. God honored Elijah's faith and his anointing. As long as the prophet used the anointing for the work of the Lord, he could expect to get results.

Now we turn our attention to Elisha. It is evident that Elisha believed in the anointing. Before he ever operated in the anointing with people, he tested it at the Jordan River.

Elijah and Elisha had crossed over the river together on dry ground. As Elijah was caught up into heaven to be with the younger prophet no more, Elisha took up Elijah's mantle, which represented the anointing. Immediately Elisha took the mantle to the edge of the Jordan River and struck the water with it as he cried out, **Where is the Lord God of Elijah?** (2 Kings 2:14).

The water parted in response to Elisha's faith, just as it had done for Elijah. The knowledge that the anointing of God was upon him just as he had asked gave Elisha great confidence in the anointing God had placed on his life, as we see demonstrated in Second Kings 4:1-3 NKJV:

> A certain woman of the wives of the sons of the prophets cried out to Elisha, saying, "Your servant my husband is dead, and you know that your servant feared the LORD. And the creditor is coming to take my two sons to be his slaves."
>
> So Elisha said to her, "What shall I do for you? Tell me, what do you have in the house?" And she said, "Your maidservant has nothing in the house but a jar of oil."
>
> Then he said, "Go, borrow vessels from everywhere, from all your neighbors—empty vessels; do not gather just a few."

Elisha started out addressing the woman with a question: "What shall I do for you?" This sounds like Jesus's statement to blind Bartimaeus, "What do you want Me to do for you?" (Mark 10:51 NKJV.)

Elisha continued by giving this poor woman directions to follow. Jesus practiced this same method many times. The person's obedience to follow directions determined whether or not the anointing worked.

The same type of thing took place with Paul at Lystra when he spoke to the crippled man whom he perceived to have faith. Paul said with a loud voice, "Stand upright on thy feet." When the man did as Paul said, he was completely healed. (See Acts 14:8-10.)

When the woman followed Elisha's instructions, a miracle occurred, as recorded in 2 Kings 4:4-6 NKJV. Elisha told the woman:

> **"And when you have come in, you shall shut the door behind you and your sons; then pour it into all those vessels, and set aside the full ones."**
>
> **So she went from him and shut the door behind her and her sons, who brought the vessels to her; and she poured it out.**
>
> **Now it came to pass, when the vessels were full, that she said to her son, "Bring me another vessel." And he said to her, "There is not another vessel." So the oil ceased.**

The next case involving Elisha occurs later in chapter 4. It is the account of the Shunammite woman's son being raised from the dead.

Elisha had spoken to the Shunammite woman when she was childless, promising her that she would have a son by the same time the following year. Sure enough, according to the word of the man of God, she had a son (vv. 8-17).

Then the son became ill and died. The mother sought Elisha by saying, **"As the Lord lives, and as your soul lives, I will not leave you"** (v. 30 NKJV). This woman was *not* letting go of her miracle! So when news of the situation reached Elisha, he took action by telling his servant what to do:

> **Then he said to Gehazi, "Get yourself ready, and take my staff in your hand, and be on your way. If you meet anyone, do not greet him; and if anyone greets you, do not answer him; but lay my staff on the face of the child."**
>
> **2 Kings 4:29** NKJV

Elisha gave instructions to his servant to minister to the boy so he would live by placing the staff on the boy's face. Elisha obviously had faith that the boy would revive.

The Old Testament prophet often worked this way. The practice of laying his staff on the sick person's body could be likened to the laying on of hands in the church today. However, when the servant did as Elisha had instructed, the boy's lifeless body didn't respond.

It is amazing to me that Elisha believed the boy would be raised from the dead by the laying on of his staff. Elisha wasn't just trying something to stall for time. He was working the works of God. He didn't seem rattled when the boy failed to come back from the dead, but he did become more focused.

When Elisha arrived on the scene himself, he went into the room where the boy lay and shut the door behind him. Then he prayed to the Lord (vv. 31-33).

Can you see the strength of what was happening? Elisha believed so deeply in the anointing of God that he worked the anointing himself with full intentions of raising that boy from the dead! It didn't seem to cross Elisha's mind at all that the child would not get up; the prophet just seemed to realize that there was another way to raise him.

The Lord revealed to Elisha what to do, and Elisha obeyed. The prophet lay down on the child twice—and the child was restored to life (vv. 34-37).

Do you think it helped Elisha in this situation to have earlier witnessed Elijah raise the widow's son from the dead? Sure it did. It raised his consciousness to believe it was possible.

How we believe God to work with us and through us makes all the difference in the world.

Here are three more examples of times when Elisha operated the anointing:

> **And Elisha returned to Gilgal, and there was a famine in the land. Now the sons of the prophets were sitting before him; and he said to his servant, "Put on the large pot, and boil stew for the sons of the prophets."**
>
> **So one went out into the field to gather herbs, and found a wild vine, and gathered from it a lapful of wild gourds, and came and sliced them**

into the pot of stew, though they did not know what they were.

Then they served it to the men to eat. Now it happened, as they were eating the stew, that they cried out and said, "Man of God, there is death in the pot!" And they could not eat it.

So he said, "Then bring some flour." And he put it into the pot, and said, "Serve it to the people, that they may eat." And there was nothing harmful in the pot.

2 Kings 4:38-41 NKJV

As you can see, when the pot became poisonous, the people who were eating from it immediately conferred with the man of God about what to do. Elisha responded, "Bring me some flour."

Elisha wasn't asking for some kind of special flour that kills all harmful bacteria. He simply said, "Bring me some flour." There wasn't a word of the Lord in this situation; it was just Elisha's plan. He was a man of God with the anointing, and he knew that the anointing would work with him.

As Elisha's instructions were followed, the anointing began to work. By faith, the prophet said, "Now serve the stew to the people." And when the people began to eat it, they discovered the stew had been cured.

We find a similar situation when Elisha recovered a lost ax head.

> And the sons of the prophets said to Elisha, "See now, the place where we dwell with you is too small for us.
>
> "Please, let us go to the Jordan, and let every man take a beam from there, and let us make there a place where we may dwell." So he answered, "Go."
>
> Then one said, "Please consent to go with your servants." And he answered, "I will go."
>
> So he went with them. And when they came to the Jordan, they cut down trees.
>
> But as one was cutting down a tree, the iron ax head fell into the water; and he cried out and said, "Alas, master! For it was borrowed."
>
> So the man of God said, "Where did it fall?" And he showed him the place. So he cut off a stick, and threw it in there; and he made the iron float.
>
> Therefore he said, "Pick it up for yourself." So he reached out his hand and took it.
>
> 2 Kings 6:1-7 NKJV

The ax head was lost. Nevertheless, Elijah asked, "Where did the ax fall?"

No, the prophet wasn't getting ready to put on a snorkel, plunge into the water, and start searching the bottom of the river. Instead, he grabbed a stick from a tree and walked over to the spot where the ax fell in.

Why a stick? Let's figure it out. If the anointing can abide in a staff, which is wood, it can also get into a little twig.

Elisha threw the stick into the water at the right place. He put the anointing on the spot, and the miracle took place. There was no word of the Lord involved in this instance. Elisha had simply learned how God would work with him.

What would we have done? Would we have gathered everyone together to see if there was enough money to run to the corner hardware store and buy another ax head? Would we have pulled out our credit card without thinking and charged it?

I think this is a tremendous example of a creative mind who only knows how to win with God's help. But such examples shouldn't be limited to Bible characters like Elisha. Surely if an Old Testament prophet can learn to work with God, New Testament sons of God can do the same!

Like Elisha, we are co-laborers with God. God works with us, and we work with Him for the ultimate good of His plan. Note this: We are never in a competition to produce results in one particular way versus another. The end results in the ministry of Jesus were all the same. How He achieved those results varied according to each situation.

Consider one more example from Elisha's ministry. This passage is different from the ones we just studied, yet the results are ultimately the same.

> **Then a man came from Baal Shalisha, and brought the man of God bread of the firstfruits, twenty loaves of barley bread, and newly ripened grain in his knapsack. And he said, "Give it to the people, that they may eat."**
>
> **But his servant said, "What? Shall I set this before one hundred men?" He said again, "Give it to the people, that they may eat; for thus says the LORD: 'They shall eat and have some left over.'"**
>
> **So he set it before them; and they ate and had some left over, according to the word of the LORD.**
>
> **2 Kings 4:42-44 NKJV**

Here the word of the Lord led Elisha to perform a miracle of increase. As the prophet's instructions were followed, the anointing produced an increase of the barley bread.

All the necessary components were present in this situation, just as before. The words were just as anointed. The only difference was in the fact that the instructions were initiated from a different source. However, if we consider the fact that Elisha's will was completely submitted to the will of God, we can see that the source of both miracles was really one and the same.

The same should be true in our lives. We are one with Christ, after all, we have the mind of Christ. Therefore, as we work in faith with the anointing God has given us, we must seriously endeavor to be led by God and to follow His heart at all times. We have no license to make up a "word" to see if it will work. We are acutally learning to think like God for the ultimate benefit of establishing God's will.

BE BOLD *IN GOD*

As you allow God to use you in demonstrations of His power, I recommend that you begin as the Lord started with me. At first, wait until you hear the word of the Lord. Let the Lord tutor you and show you how He will work with you. Remember, the Holy Ghost is in you to teach you and to guide you as you keep your heart fixed on Him.

I want to relate one of the ways God has worked with me along this line. Perhaps this illustration will help you learn how to better walk in the fullness of who you are and what you have in Christ.

Working in a healing school every day is very

demanding. I had to rely on the Holy Ghost all the time for His unction in order to know what to say and do. After all, what would healing school be without healings? Just school.

I have always had a drive to succeed; therefore, I have relied on God to help me so the people who attended the healing school would be healed and God would be ultimately glorified.

God began to give me revelations that I have shared in this book and other truths I will later write about in a book on *Living in the Miraculous*. The direction the Lord led me in the Word gradually produced great boldness and a confident knowledge that if I did my part, He would do His.

First, I started with the blood covenant. I saw how God had bound Himself to the terms of the covenant. I realized He did this so we could have bold and daring faith in His willingness and ability to perform the Word on our behalf.

The stronger I preached and taught, the more the Holy Ghost encouraged me to be even bolder. I didn't think it was possible. I would do the best I could, and each time more would happen. But then the Lord would again say, *"Be bolder!"*

I continued to learn truths from God's Word that provided me with a strong platform for greater boldness. The further the Lord led me, the more results were produced.

One day the Lord said something to me that really shocked me. As I was walking out of my office door to go to the healing school service, I asked God, "What am I going to say today that I haven't already said?" I felt as if I didn't know what else to do.

Then I heard the Lord's audible voice speak from behind me. He said, "Whatever you do, I will back you up."

I turned around to see who had said that. Once again the Lord said, "Whatever you do, I will back you up."

I said, "Lord, You didn't say, whatever *I do*, did You?"

For the third time, I heard the Lord say, "Whatever you do, I will back you up."

As I went out the door to the service, I immediately felt I had risen to a different position in God. I wasn't so afraid to risk missing God by stepping out in faith. That personal word from the Lord in my office gave me new confidence that He would work with me as I worked with Him.

Days later I was pondering these same thoughts. As I was once more walking out the door to go to the service, I said, "Lord, today there will be at least two people healed before the service is over." Did I say that in response to a word from the Lord? No, I just said it by faith.

Do you think God has a problem working with someone who by faith desires to do the same things He sent Jesus to do? Of course He doesn't.

At the beginning of the service I boldly said to the congregation, "Before the service is over today, you will see at least two people healed."

As I preached, I continued to repeat myself to the people. Halfway through the service, I decided the time had come, so I said, "Right now the first person will be healed."

I looked at a woman sitting in the front row and asked her, "Do you want to be the first one?"

"Yes," she replied.

At the time, it didn't seem as if I was being led by the Holy Spirit. But by the time I finish with this story, you will see that the Lord was indeed directing me to step out in faith in this way.

This woman had suffered from a muscular disease for at least fifteen years. She had endured nonstop pain for that entire time. I barely touched her forehead, and the joy on her face told the story. She was instantly healed, and we glorified God.

This was on a Wednesday. Normally on Thursday, we laid hands on the sick in healing school.

So I said to this woman, "Tomorrow we will be laying hands on the sick. If you need anything else, come tomorrow, and I will lay hands on you again." (Now, I know I didn't have to do it that way, but that is how I spoke to this woman on that particular day.)

She said, "Today was the only day I could come."

Of course, we were delighted that she was healed on the one day she *could* come!

I continued to preach, and about fifteen minutes later I pointed to another woman and asked, "Do you want to be the second one to be healed today?"

"Yes," the woman responded.

So I asked her, "What do you need healing for?"

The woman explained that she had bone spurs on the bottom of her feet that caused her excruciating pain. Without batting an eye, I told the woman, "Step out in the aisle, pick up your foot, and slam it into the floor. As you do, you will be healed."

The woman did as I instructed and was totally healed!

We all rejoiced again; then I said to the woman, "Tomorrow we will lay hands on the sick. If you need anything else, come tomorrow."

Like the first woman who had been healed, this second woman replied, "Today was the only day I could come."

Consider how much God wanted to heal those two women! What if I had not taken my position to believe and expect results?

It is likely that I wouldn't have personally ministered healing to anyone that day, and they would have gone home without their healing. Do you see how God was working with me so I could tap into His ultimate plan for healing school that day and do the works of Jesus?

Friend, I challenge you to do what God requires you to do to get out of your box of limited expectations, if you haven't already done so. Determine to leave behind religion and to discover how God wants to be God in your life today.

Get excited about what God is doing on this earth and what He wants to do through you. God is no respecter of persons. Others are going forth and doing the works of Jesus for God's glory and others' benefit—and *so can you*!

CONCLUSION

I want to personally thank you for investing your time in this material. The pages you have just read were written to challenge you to be all that God has intended for you to be. They were written from a deep sense of urgency, for never has there been such a critical time in history. Never has there been such a need for the finished work of Christ to be implemented in this earth. To be sure, people's intentions have been good and their hearts have been pure; yet the work of the Lord has lacked in application.

That leaves us with this question: Would we be proud to stand in the presence of Jesus as we are? Perhaps we could show Him all the projects we have completed and all the good things we have done. But what about the eternal trophies—the ones that come from the souls who are touched for God and from the divine call that has been fulfilled the way it was given through the heart of God?

Jude exhorted us to *contend earnestly* for the faith. (Jude.) He wasn't talking about just any faith, but the faith that once was given to the saints—faith that Jesus demonstrated in His ministry.

It is so important that we experience and utilize the fullness of our equipment in God, but we can only do that as we contend earnestly for Jesus's kind of faith to be demonstrated in our lives. We can only know God's fullness as we determine to be bold, courageous, and strong in Him.

A great man of God once said that in the Spirit, he could hear the sound of God searching throughout His troops for those who would display boldness—boldness to preach the Word and boldness to move with the Spirit of God. God's call for boldness is still beckoning the hearts of men today.

Who will rise up and be held accountable for the task at hand? Will you? Until He comes, you are the answer to the needs of this world. Will you believe it? Will you accept it?

If you want to experience the fullness of God, my friend, you must first accept the mandate of God. He is calling you right now, saying, "Know who you are; know what you have; and know what you can and must do—*until I come!*"

SCRIPTURES TO LIVE BY

The following scriptures are (all from the NKJV) are some of Jesus's thoughts that caused God's life and power to continually flow in Him and through Him to others. To apply these Scriptures to your lives, meditate on them, speak boldly about them, and prepare yourself to act as though these Scriptures are fulfilled through you. If Jesus thought it, so must we. If He spoke it, so must we. And if He lived it, we must be willing to say, "So be it—let it live in me!"

In Him was life, and the life was the light of men.

And the light shines in the darkness, and the darkness did not comprehend it.

John 1:4-5

But as many as received Him, to them He gave the right to become children of God, to those who believe in His name:

who were born, not of blood, nor of the will of the flesh, nor of the will of man, but of God.

John 1:12-13

And of His fullness we have all received, and grace for grace.

John 1:16

No one has seen God at any time. The only begotten Son, who is in the bosom of the Father, He has declared Him.

John 1:18

Since Jesus declared the Father to the world, so must we declare or introduce Jesus to the world.

"Most assuredly, I say to you, We speak what We know and testify what We have seen, and you do not receive Our witness."

John 3:11

Jesus said to them, "My food is to do the will of Him who sent Me, and to finish His work."

John 4:34

But Jesus answered them, "My Father has been working until now, and I have been working."

John 5:17

"For as the Father raises the dead and gives life to them, even so the Son gives life to whom He will."

John 5:21

"Most assuredly, I say to you, he who hears My word and believes in Him who sent Me has everlasting life, and shall not come into judgment, but has passed from death into life."

John 5:24

"For as the Father has life in Himself, so He has granted the Son to have life in Himself,
    "and has given Him authority to execute judgment also, because He is the Son of Man."

John 5:26-27

If you have eternal life, you are automatically authorized to execute judgment over the works of the devil.

"It is the Spirit who gives life; the flesh profits nothing. The words that I speak to you are spirit, and they are life."

John 6:63

Jesus answered them and said, "My doctrine is not Mine, but His who sent Me."

John 7:16

"But I know Him, for I am from Him, and He sent Me."

John 7:29

"He who believes in Me, as the Scripture has said, out of his heart will flow rivers of living water."

John 7:38

And He said to them, "You are from beneath; I am from above. You are of this world; I am not of this world."

John 8:23

"And He who sent Me is with Me. The Father has not left Me alone, for I always do those things that please Him."

John 8:29

Jesus said to them, "If God were your Father, you would love Me, for I proceeded forth and came from God; nor have I come of Myself, but He sent Me."

John 8:42

"He who is of God hears God's words; therefore you do not hear, because you are not of God."

John 8:47

"Yet you have not known Him, but I know Him. And if I say, 'I do not know Him,' I shall be a liar like you; but I do know Him and keep His word."

John 8:55

Jesus answered, "Neither this man nor his parents sinned, but that the works of God should be revealed in him.

"I must work the works of Him who sent Me while it is day; the night is coming when no one can work.

"As long as I am in the world, I am the light of the world."

John 9:3-5

"My sheep hear My voice, and I know them, and they follow Me."

John 10:27

"If I do not do the works of My Father, do not believe Me;

"but if I do, though you do not believe Me, believe the works, that you may know and believe that the Father is in Me, and I in Him."

John 10:37-38

"For I have not spoken on My own authority; but the Father who sent Me gave Me a command, what I should say and what I should speak.

"And I know that His command is everlasting life. Therefore, whatever I speak, just as the Father has told Me, so I speak."

John 12:49-50

"If you had known Me, you would have known My Father also; and from now on you know Him and have seen Him."

John 14:7

"Most assuredly, I say to you, he who believes in Me, the works that I do he will do also; and greater works than these he will do, because I go to My Father.

"And whatever you ask in My name, that I will do, that the Father may be glorified in the Son.

"If you ask anything in My name, I will do it."

John 14:12-14

And I will pray the Father, and He will give you another Helper, that He may abide with you forever,

"even the Spirit of truth, whom the world cannot receive, because it neither sees Him nor knows Him; but you know Him, for He dwells with you and will be in you."

John 14:16-17

"At that day you will know that I am in My Father, and you in Me, and I in you."

John 14:20

"I am the true vine, and My Father is the vine-dresser.

"Every branch in Me that does not bear fruit He takes away; and every branch that bears fruit He prunes, that it may bear more fruit.

"You are already clean because of the word which I have spoken to you.

"Abide in Me, and I in you. As the branch cannot bear fruit of itself, unless it abides in the vine, neither can you, unless you abide in Me.

"I am the vine, you are the branches. He who abides in Me, and I in him, bears much fruit; for without Me you can do nothing."

John 15:1-5

"If you were of the world, the world would love its own. Yet because you are not of the world, but I chose you out of the world, therefore the world hates you."

John 15:19

"But when the Helper comes, whom I shall send to you from the Father, the Spirit of truth who proceeds from the Father, He will testify of Me.

"And you also will bear witness, because you have been with Me from the beginning."

John 15:26-27

"Nevertheless I tell you the truth. It is to your advantage that I go away; for if I do not go away, the Helper will not come to you; but if I depart, I will send Him to you."

John 16:7

"However, when He, the Spirit of truth, has come, He will guide you into all truth; for He will not speak on His own authority, but whatever He hears He will speak; and He will tell you things to come."

John 16:13

"They are not of the world, just as I am not of the world."

John 17:16

"I do not pray for these alone, but also for those who will believe in Me through their word;

"that they all may be one, as You, Father, are in Me, and I in You; that they also may be one in Us, that the world may believe that You sent Me."

John 17:20-21

"And I have declared to them Your name, and will declare it, that the love with which You loved Me may be in them, and I in them."

John 17:26

You are one with Jesus. Therefore, let this mind be in you that was also in Him!

ENDNOTES

1 Clarence Jordan, *The Cotton Patch Version of Paul's Epistles* (New York, NY: Association Press, 1968).

2 John G. Lake, *The Complete Collection of His Life Teachings* (Tulsa, OK: Albury Publishing, 1999), p. 502.

3 *The Distilled Bible/New Testament* (Stone Mountain, GA: Paul Benjamin Co., 1980).

4 *Webster's New Students Dictionary, Teachers Annotated Edition* (Springfield, MA: G & C Merriam Co., 1969), p. 215.

5 *The Online Bible Thayer's Greek Lexicon* and *Brown, Driver & Briggs' Hebrew Lexicon* (Ontario, Canada: Woodside Bible Fellowship, licensed from the Institute for Creation Research, 1993).

6 *Biblesoft's New Exhaustive Strong's Numbers and Concordance with Expanded Greek-Hebrew Dictionary,* (Biblesoft and International Bible Translators, Inc., 1994), No. 2205.

7 W. E. Vine, *Vine's Expository Dictionary of Biblical Words* (Nashville, TN.: Thomas Nelson Publishers, 1985), p. 332.

8 *The Online Bible: Thayer's Greek Lexicon and Brown Driver, and Briggs' Hebrew Lexicon* (Ontario, Canada: Woodside Bible Fellowship, 1993).

9 *Webster's New Students Dictionary, Teachers Annotated Edition* (Springfield, MA: G & C Merriam Co., 1969), p. 163.

10 Ibid., p. 27.

11 *Biblesoft's New Exhaustive Strong's Numbers and Concordance with Expanded Greek-Hebrew Dictionary* (Biblesoft and International Bible Translators, Inc., 1994), No. 1849.

12 *The Online Bible: Thayer's Greek Lexicon and Brown, Driver, and Briggs' Hebrew Lexicon* (Ontario, Canada: Woodside Bible Fellowship, 1993).

13 W. E. Vine, *Vine's Expository Dictionary of Biblical Words* (Nashville, TN: Thomas Nelson Publishers, 1985), pp. 680-681.

ABOUT THE AUTHOR

J im Hockaday was raised in a Christian home where he was born again at four years of age. He experienced the call of God on his life and the desire to preach even in these early years.

After graduating from Wheaton College in 1983, he traveled and ministered with several Christian music groups, including the Spurlows, Truth, and the Living Word Singers.

When God put in Jim's heart a strong desire to know more of Him, he attended Rhema Bible Training Center and graduated in 1988. Immediately following graduation, he joined the Rhema Singers and Band and traveled extensively with Rev. Kenneth E. Hagin and the group for nearly seven years.

Jim has been the Coordinator of Prayer and Healing School for Kenneth Hagin Ministries, ministering daily in both Prayer School and Healing School from 1994 to 2004. It has been Jim's heart's desire to assist others in developing a vivid relationship with God. When a ministry begins to resemble the ministry of Jesus, the next step is to teach and mentor others to do the same. This need has been the passion and motivation behind the call on Jim's life.

In 1991, Jim founded Jim Hockaday Ministries, Inc. Through the years, he has traveled and ministered in churches both in the United States and abroad. He has also been privileged to travel to and minister in several Rhema Bible Training Centers around the world.

Jim resides in the Tulsa area with his wife Erin (a 1991 graduate of Rhema Bible Training Center and a former member of The Rhema Singers and Band for two and a half years), and their young daughters Alli, Drew, and Chloe.